° THE °
CHILDREN'S
ATLAS OF
WORLD
HISTORY

Photographs Front cover: wood carving found in Viking ship grave, in Norway; Persian miniature showing Chinghiz Khan; temple-pyramid at Chichén Itzá, in Mexico; Victorian cartoon of European powers sharing out China; back cover: early Chinese bronze vessel; the Sphinx and Great Pyramid in Giza, in Egypt; terracotta plaque of Hindu goddess; previous page: painting of Chinese magistrates; opposite page: ruins of Machu Picchu in Peru.

Published in the United States in 1999 by Peter Bedrick Books
A division of NTC/Contemporary Publishing Group, Inc.
4255 West Touhy Avenue
Lincolnwood (Chicago), Illinois 60646-1975 U.S.A.

© 1997 Horus Editions

Text by Neil DeMarco BA, MA
Text consultant Dr Kendrick Oliver
Project editor Elizabeth A Miles
Designed by Richard Rowan
Additional design by Edward Kinsey
Maps by Janos Marffy and John Downes
Illustrations by Chris Rothero, Ian Heard and John Downes

Library of Congress Cataloging-in-Publication Data

DeMarco, Neil.
    The children's atlas of world history / Neil DeMarco.
        p.   cm.
    Originally published: London: Horus Editions, 1997.
    Includes index.
    Summary: A history of the world, from the birth of civilization to modern times, featuring maps and time charts.
    ISBN 0-87226-603-6
    1. World history Atlases Juvenile literature.   2. Children's atlases. [1. World history Atlases.   2. Atlases.]   I. Title.
    D21.5.D42   1999
    911—dc21

99-29940
CIP

Printed and bound in Singapore

International Standard Book Number: 0-87226-603-6

The heading strips in this book illustrate aspects of the history explored on each page, as follows:

Page 5 digging for historical evidence at an archaeological site; p6 hunting woolly mammoth; p8 an early settlement; p12 an early Mesopotamian city; p14 pyramids at Giza on the Nile; p16 a grain store in the Indus valley; p18 warring bands in early China; p20 King Darius I hunting a lion; p22 the Acropolis, Athens; p24 a Roman legion on the march; p28 the crucifixion; p30 the city of Constantinople; p32 Muslims at prayer; p34 the cavalry of the Carolingians; p36 Vikings landing and raiding a village; p38 a medieval castle; p40 a Japanese Buddhist pagoda; p42 soldiers on the Great Wall of China; p44 Mongols and their tents on a plain; p46 an African mosque; p48 playing ball in Mayan times; p52 the ships of Christopher Columbus; p54 fighting in the Thirty Years War; p56 the Kremlin, Moscow; p58 a scene at the Persian court; p60 the Chinese emperor on tour; p62 the shogun Tokugawa Ieyasu; p64 a British fort on the coast of India; p68 an early steam engine; p70 the storming of the Bastille; p72 Bolivar and the Battle of Carabobo, Venezuela; p74 a wagon-train of settlers heading westward; p76 an early industrial landscape; p 78 smoking opium in China; p82 French soldiers in the Verdun; p84 Allied bombers in flight; p86 independence ceremony in Nigeria; p88 telecommunications dish and satellite.

◦ THE ◦
CHILDREN'S
ATLAS OF
WORLD
HISTORY

PETER BEDRICK BOOKS
NEW YORK

CONTENTS

INTRODUCTION **5**
THE FIRST MEN AND WOMEN 6
THE FIRST FARMERS 8

ANCIENT CIVILIZATIONS AND EMPIRES **10**
CITIES AND EMPIRES OF MESOPOTAMIA 12
ANCIENT EGYPT 14
INDIAN CIVILIZATIONS 16
CIVILIZATIONS IN EARLY CHINA 18
THE PERSIAN EMPIRE 20
GREEK CIVILIZATIONS 22
THE ROMAN EMPIRE 24

THE MIDDLE AGES **26**
THE SPREAD OF CHRISTIANITY 28
THE BYZANTINE EMPIRE 30
THE SPREAD OF ISLAM 32
BARBARIAN EUROPE 34
THE VIKING EXPANSION 36
MEDIEVAL EUROPE 38
THE SPREAD OF BUDDHISM 40
MEDIEVAL CHINA 42
THE MONGOL EXPANSION 44
AFRICAN KINGDOMS 46
NATIVE EMPIRES OF AMERICA 48

EMPIRES AROUND THE WORLD **50**
PORTUGUESE AND SPANISH EMPIRES 52
RELIGION AND DEVELOPMENT IN EUROPE 54
THE EXPANSION OF RUSSIA 56
NEW ISLAMIC EMPIRES 58
THE EXPANSION OF CHINA 60
JAPAN IN WAR AND PEACE 62
EUROPEANS IN ASIA AND THE PACIFIC 64

INDUSTRY AND REVOLUTION **66**
THE INDUSTRIAL REVOLUTION 68
THE FRENCH REVOLUTION 70
INDEPENDENCE IN LATIN AMERICA 72
THE EXPANSION OF THE UNITED STATES 74
NATION STATES IN EUROPE 76
THE DECLINE OF CHINA 78

THE TWENTIETH CENTURY **80**
THE FIRST WORLD WAR 82
THE SECOND WORLD WAR 84
INDEPENDENCE IN ASIA AND AFRICA 86
TOWARD A NEW CENTURY 88
GLOSSARY AND INDEX **90**

INTRODUCTION

HISTORY IS THE study of the people and events of the past. The study includes three elements. First, historians try to find out how people lived, what happened to them, and what happened around them. Second, historians search for the reasons behind these events. Third, they examine the effects, or consequences, of the events. Historians do not only describe the facts of history. They also give their views, or interpretations, of events. Often historians hold different views, which makes history even more interesting. It also explains why so many different books are written about the same historical subjects (each writer brings a different point of view to the subject). However, all historians must follow one golden rule in their approach to the past: they must base their interpretations of events on the evidence. Anything that tells us about the past is evidence, such as written documents, art, coins, tools and buildings.

Herodotus
Herodotus (c.484–424 BC) of Ancient Greece traveled widely in Asia, Europe and Egypt. He is called the "Father of History" because as he traveled he wrote down oral accounts of past events, peoples and places in the areas he visited. In his nine-book account of the Greek-Persian wars of the 5th century BC, he not only told what happened, but he also tried to explain why it happened.

Dating the past
The system used for dating the past in this book is one that developed in the Christian world. All years before the birth of Christ are known as BC, Before Christ. The years after are called AD, an abbreviation for the Latin words *anno domini*, which mean "in the year of Our Lord." So AD 1 is the first year after the birth of Christ. A date in the 1st century after the birth of Christ is one between AD 1 and 100. Non-Christian peoples, such as the Jews, Muslims and Chinese, have their own calendars. But the system described above is the one most commonly used in the world today for dating the past.

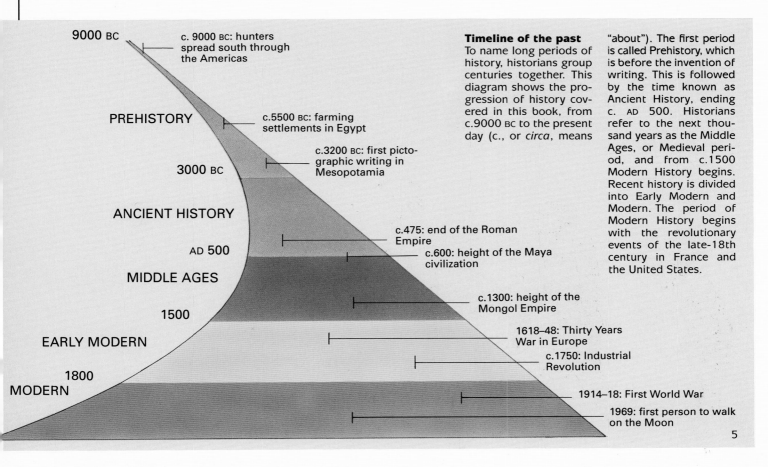

9000 BC

c. 9000 BC: hunters spread south through the Americas

PREHISTORY

c.5500 BC: farming settlements in Egypt

3000 BC

c.3200 BC: first pictographic writing in Mesopotamia

ANCIENT HISTORY

c.475: end of the Roman Empire

AD 500

c.600: height of the Maya civilization

MIDDLE AGES

c.1300: height of the Mongol Empire

1500

1618–48: Thirty Years War in Europe

EARLY MODERN

c.1750: Industrial Revolution

1800
MODERN

1914–18: First World War

1969: first person to walk on the Moon

Timeline of the past
To name long periods of history, historians group centuries together. This diagram shows the progression of history covered in this book, from c.9000 BC to the present day (c., or *circa*, means "about"). The first period is called Prehistory, which is before the invention of writing. This is followed by the time known as Ancient History, ending c. AD 500. Historians refer to the next thousand years as the Middle Ages, or Medieval period, and from c.1500 Modern History begins. Recent history is divided into Early Modern and Modern. The period of Modern History begins with the revolutionary events of the late-18th century in France and the United States.

THE FIRST MEN AND WOMEN

H UMAN BEINGS, like all forms of life, have been created by a long process of development, called evolution. We are most like two of the great apes, the gorilla and the chimpanzee. We differ from them in that we always walk upright on two legs and have much larger brains. The first creatures which resembled human beings appeared in Africa, and we call them *Australopithecus*, which means "southern ape." They lived between 5 and 1.5 million years ago. Our direct ancestors evolved about 2.3 million years ago, also in Africa, and we call them *Homo*, which means "man." They were more clearly human than their ancestors, had much bigger brains, and could make tools. There have been four main types of *Homo*. *Homo sapiens sapiens* is the most recent type of human.

Power through tools
One of the reasons humans became such successful animals was that they developed tools. Tools were made from stone, bone, wood and antlers. Early stone tools were made by knocking one stone against another stone. One of the stones was cut away on two sides which gave it sharp edges. Their main use was for carving up dead animals for their meat and skins. *Homo sapiens* later developed a wide range of tools, which they used in different ways to make their lives easier.

Early types of human
The four main types of humans are *Homo habilis*, *Homo erectus*, *Homo sapiens*, and *Homo sapiens sapiens* (modern humans). Many fossil bones of early humans have been found in Africa and we can tell from these bones what they were like. Each new type of human walked more upright than the one before. They also developed larger, more intelligent brains. See below from left to right: the first Australopithecine; *Homo habilis*, who made the first stone tools; and *Homo sapiens*. *Homo sapiens sapiens* evolved about 100,000 years ago and spread rapidly across the globe. The one below carries a stick, and a spear, which he would have used for hunting.

The spread of modern people
The way in which people spread around the world was affected by climate. *Homo erectus* spread out from Africa into southern Europe, southeast Asia and east Asia. They could not settle in northern America or northern Europe because these areas were covered in thick sheets of ice. *Homo sapiens sapiens*, however, did spread to all parts of the world, between 90,000 and 30,000 years ago. They moved up into northern Europe and into Asia. From there they traveled on foot and by primitive boats or rafts to Australia, where they settled at least 50,000 years ago. The first inhabitants of North and South America probably walked from Siberia to Alaska and down through America about 30,000 years ago. This is why the native peoples of North and South America look rather like the people of east Asia. As *Homo sapiens sapiens* settled in various parts

Key

coastline of about 16,000 BC

places where evidence of *Homo sapiens sapiens* has been found, from these periods:

100,000 – 71,000 BC

70,000 – 46,000 BC

45,000 – 26,000 BC

25,000 – 16,000 BC

15,000 – 8,000 BC

directions in which *Homo sapiens sapiens* spread

0   2,000 Miles

0   3,000 Km

EUROPE

AFRICA

ATLANTIC OCEAN

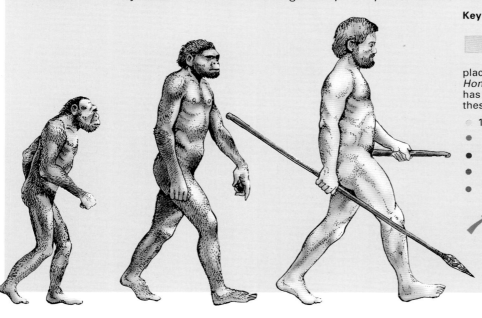

Hunters and gatherers
From about 1.5 million years ago our human ancestors developed a pattern of life called hunting and gathering. This remained the usual way of life until people invented farming, or agriculture, about 9,000 years ago. There are people, such as some of the people of the Kalahari desert in Africa, who are still hunter-gatherers. Their way of life gives us some idea of how our ancestors may have hunted and gathered food. They form small groups of about 25 people, and each group moves about from camp to camp within its own territory. The women gather most of the food, such as melons, seeds and insects. The men hunt large animals, such as the gemsbok antelope carried by the men in this picture.

The world's oldest paintings
Homo sapiens sapiens produced the world's first art about 35,000 years ago. They used the surface of cave walls to paint on, and produced small sculptures. So far over 100 caves with prehistoric paintings have been discovered. The oldest of these are in southwest Africa. Many have also been found in southwest France and northeast Spain. Most of the paintings show animals, such as bison, oxen and horses, as in these beautiful paintings at Lascaux, in southern France. They were hidden in dark caves and could only have been seen with a flame. So why did these early humans paint them? Some experts have suggested that they believed the paintings gave them magical help during their hunting expeditions.

of the world they adapted to the different climates and their bodies and skin color began to change. This is why there are so many different types of human beings in the world today.

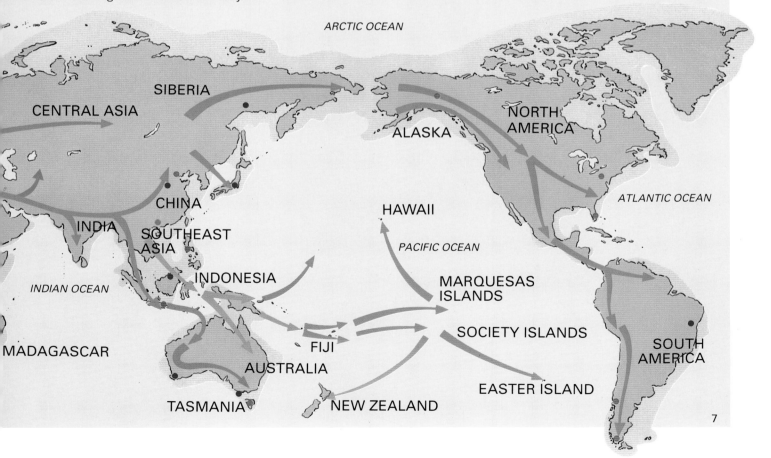

ARCTIC OCEAN

SIBERIA

CENTRAL ASIA

NORTH AMERICA

ALASKA

CHINA

HAWAII

ATLANTIC OCEAN

INDIA

SOUTHEAST ASIA

PACIFIC OCEAN

INDONESIA

MARQUESAS ISLANDS

INDIAN OCEAN

MADAGASCAR

FIJI

SOCIETY ISLANDS

SOUTH AMERICA

AUSTRALIA

EASTER ISLAND

TASMANIA

NEW ZEALAND

THE FIRST FARMERS

FOR ABOUT TWO million years, generations of men and women spent their lives on the move, hunting and gathering. However, from about 11,000 years ago (9000 BC) a new way of life based on agriculture developed. This eventually became a much more common way of life than hunting and gathering.

Agricultural life first appeared in the Middle East, where people discovered they could grow the grains of certain wild grasses outside their normal growing areas and produce more food. Now they no longer had to wander around collecting food. They could live together in one place because farming provided enough food to feed everyone. So villages appeared for the first time. In the next 4,000 years the same thing began to happen in South America, Central America, India and China.

Works of art in bronze
After agriculture and pot-making, the next important development in early-human life was metalworking. This happened at different times around the world (see map). At first, just copper and gold were hammered to make objects. Later, copper was mixed with tin to produce bronze. Later still, iron was discovered. This was a common metal, used for items needing strength, such as swords. In northern Europe bronze was used between 2300 and 700 BC. This bronze work of art was made in about 650 BC.

The use of animals in fields
As people discovered how to grow crops and village life began, they also learned how to tame animals and keep them in or near their villages. From these domesticated animals they got products such as milk and wool. In the Middle East the earliest domesticated animals were goats, sheep, cattle and pigs. In South America it was different – they had guinea pigs, llamas and alpacas.

Following the invention of the plow, cattle became very important. A plow is a piece of wood pulled through the soil, opening up furrows which let in the air. Cattle are used to pull plows. Plowing makes the soil more fertile, which means the crops are more plentiful and healthy. With cattle and plows the first villages grew in size as more people could be fed.

Pot-making
Pot-making was important to village life. The pots gave villagers something in which they could store food. Pot-making began at different times in different places (see map). At first, people rolled out strips of moist clay which they coiled into pots. In the Middle East, in about 3500 BC, some potters began to shape their vessels on a potter's wheel. This meant much finer pots could be made.

Stonehenge

The people of the Middle East began to move into Europe in about 6000 BC. Over the next 3,000 years their village way of life spread out across Europe. In southeast Europe, villages were built with houses made of mud-bricks. In other areas wood and thatch were the main building materials. In many parts of Europe villagers chopped down forests to make room for fields to grow crops.

When people died their bodies were treated with respect by the new settlers in Europe. They built tombs for the dead, made of huge stones called "megaliths." Thousands of these can still

be seen around Europe today. Between 3200 and 1500 BC, the same people also built religious monuments, especially in Brittany in northwest France, and in Britain and Ireland. They were made of large stones, laid out in rows or circles. The largest and most spectacular of these monuments is Stonehenge, in southern Britain. It was probably built between 2800 and 1500 BC. Some of the stones used at Stonehenge may have been brought from mountains in south Wales – over 125 miles away! It is possible that these stones were transported by sea and river and then on sleds overland.

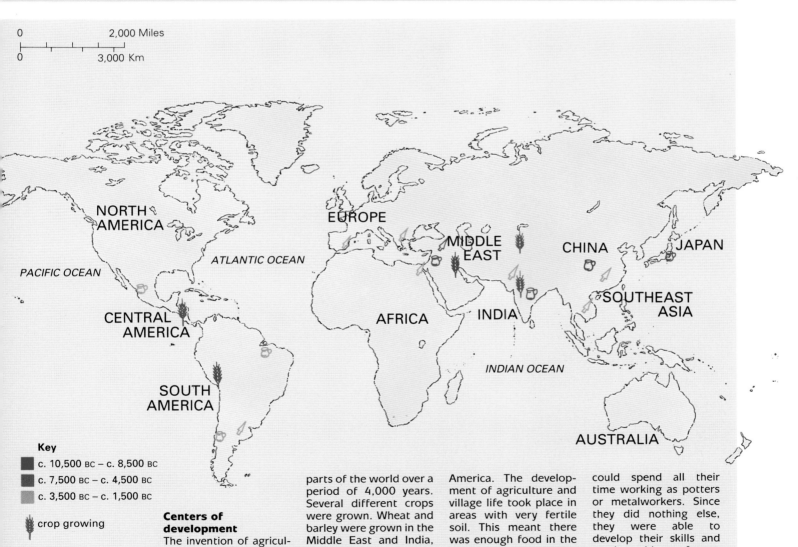

0 ⊢——⊢——⊢ 2,000 Miles
0 ⊢—⊢—⊢—⊢—⊢—⊢ 3,000 Km

NORTH AMERICA

EUROPE

MIDDLE EAST

CHINA

JAPAN

ATLANTIC OCEAN

PACIFIC OCEAN

CENTRAL AMERICA

AFRICA

INDIA

SOUTHEAST ASIA

SOUTH AMERICA

INDIAN OCEAN

AUSTRALIA

Key

- ■ c. 10,500 BC – c. 8,500 BC
- ■ c. 7,500 BC – c. 4,500 BC
- ■ c. 3,500 BC – c. 1,500 BC

🌾 crop growing

🏺 pottery

⚒ metal working

Centers of development

The invention of agriculture and the start of village life happened in perhaps five different parts of the world over a period of 4,000 years. Several different crops were grown. Wheat and barley were grown in the Middle East and India, potatoes and peppers in South America, millet in China and corn in Central America. The development of agriculture and village life took place in areas with very fertile soil. This meant there was enough food in the villages to allow some people living in them not to farm at all. They could spend all their time working as potters or metalworkers. Since they did nothing else, they were able to develop their skills and produce objects of great quality.

9

ANCIENT CIVILIZATIONS AND EMPIRES

From the beginnings of civilization in the cities of Mesopotamia to the great Roman Empire that ruled the known Western world.

EUROPE

- Western Europe has progressed from hunter-gathering to settled farming.
- In the Balkans there is evidence of advanced metalworking.
- In Varna, Bulgaria, 280 graves contain several thousand pieces of gold – the oldest gold treasure in the world.

- The Bronze Age begins in parts of northern Europe, overlapping with the Stone Age. Skills with bronze develop first in areas rich in tin.
- Much forest is cut down and the land farmed. Villagers can produce enough food to support a number of craftsmen who have different skills.

- From c.3200 to c.1500 BC people in Britain and northwest France build monuments with standing stones – in circles (Stonehenge, Britain) or in rows (Carnac, France, right). The largest stone at Carnac is over 65 feet high.
- Early Bronze Age culture begins in the Cyclades (Greek islands).

- Trading networks have been established between central and northern Europe, for metalwork and pottery.

- The Bronze Age begins in western Europe.
- On Crete the Minoan civilization flourishes, c.2200–1450 BC.

MIDDLE EAST

- The Neolithic peoples of the Middle East are the first to cultivate plants (c.9000 BC). Farming allows others to develop specialized skills. The earliest known object cast in copper was made c.5000 BC in Anatolia (Turkey). By 4000 BC animals are being domesticated.

- The world's first known cities have begun to develop in southern Mesopotamia. Merchants begin to trade in the goods produced by craftworkers. Farming techniques and irrigation systems need considerable social organization, to produce enough food for all the city's inhabitants.

- The temple at Eridu (below, left), which the Sumerians of Mesopotamia thought was the oldest city in the world.

- c.2360 BC: Sargon of Agade (below) conquers Sumer and creates an empire. It has been destroyed by c.2230 BC.

AFRICA

- Southern Africa is cut off from the more developed north by the marshes of the southern Nile Valley and the rainforest. Settled agriculture does not develop here until the Christian era.
- By 4000 BC there are settled villages in the northern Nile Valley.

- By 3500 BC Egyptians are in contact with other, neighboring countries and a common culture begins to spread over the Nile Valley and its delta plain. Simple copper tools are being used by the Egyptians, and copper and gold jewelry is buried with the dead in their tombs.

- Egypt consists of two separate kingdoms: Upper Egypt in the south and Lower Egypt in the north. The two are united into a single kingdom by King Menes, c.3100 BC, who comes from the south. He begins the First Dynasty, and rules from his new capital city at Memphis.

- c.2650 BC: the first pyramid to be made entirely of stone is built for King Djoser at Saqqarah, Egypt (below).

ASIA AND AUSTRALASIA

- A network of towns and villages has appeared along the Indus Valley, in northeast India.
- In northwest China the Yangshao people live in square or circular houses which are built partly underground and have low walls and thatched roofs. Men and women are buried separately.

- In China the first contact occurs between the Yangshao and the Longshan people of the east and northeast.

- The Longshan culture is more developed than that of the Yangshao and its people live in larger, more permanent villages.

- c.2750 BC: the Indus Valley civilization is established.
- c.2700 BC: the first bronzework in China.

- The first settlements in Melanesia in the Pacific, by peoples from Indonesia, are established by 2000 BC.

NORTH AND SOUTH AMERICA

- The peoples of the Americas have begun to grow a variety of root crops, such as potatoes and manioc.
- Animals similar to the modern llama and alpaca are being domesticated in the Andes for carrying goods and for wool, but they are not used as a major source of food.

- The peoples of Mesoamerica and Peru become better farmers (above) and can support bigger populations.

- The first settlements of five to ten houses in Mexico.
- North American Indians are making use of copper.

- An early Peruvian weaving loom (below).

- Permanent settlements of up to 4,000 people exist in Peru and there is evidence of specialized craftworkers.
- The first evidence of religion (massive platforms and ritual pits) occurs along the coast of Peru. Here the houses are made of mud, brick and stone.

By 4000 BC several important developments have taken place which create the basis for the civilizations which emerge after 4000 BC. The most important development is that people learn to grow their own crops and, instead of hunting animals for food, they begin to keep them in herds and flocks.

Villages and then cities grow up as people begin a settled way of life. The first civilizations appear along the fertile banks of major rivers such as the Euphrates and Tigris in Sumer (modern Iraq), the Nile in Egypt and the Yellow River in China. With settlement skills such as pottery and metal working evolve. Many of these civilizations also develop forms of written communication. The first writing appears in Mesopotamia.

● The Minoans trade in the Mediterranean (below).
● On the Greek mainland the dominant people are the Mycenaeans.

● 1792 BC: Hammurabi of Babylon unites Meso-potamia and founds the Babylonian Empire. This collapses c.1550 BC.

● On mainland Greece, Athens's central fortress, later known as the Acropolis, is protected by huge walls c.1300 BC.

● The Hittite Empire grows, but is destroyed by c.1200 BC by "Sea Peoples" from lands in the eastern Mediterranean.

● By 800 BC bronze work is common throughout Europe.
● Also by 800 BC the first Celtic Iron Age societies develop in Austria and Germany.
● From c.800 BC the Etruscan civilization begins in Italy.
● 753 BC: by tradition, the founding of Rome.

● From c.1000 BC a united kingdom of Israel arises under David.
● King Solomon, the son of David, dies c.930 BC and the kingdom is divided in two: Israel in the north and Judah in the south.
● King Ashurbanipal of the Assyrian Empire (below, right) feasting with his wife in a garden.

● In ancient Greece a musician playing a lyre is a decoration on a vase (below).

● 490 BC: Athens defeats the Persians at Marathon.
● 469 BC: birth of Socrates.
● 390 BC: Gauls (from modern France) capture Rome.
● 384 BC: birth of Aristotle.
● 323 BC: Alexander the Great dies, and his empire collapses.

● c.500 BC: the height of the Persian Empire. The last Persian ruler, Darius III, is defeated in 331 BC by Alexander the Great.

● In three Punic Wars between Rome and Carthage, Carthage is defeated. In the Third War, in 146 BC, Carthage is completely destroyed.
● 48 BC: Julius Caesar becomes master of Rome, but is murdered in 44 BC.
● 27 BC: Octavian becomes Augustus, emperor of Rome.

● 247 BC: the beginning of the Parthian Empire. At its height, in c.85 BC, the empire stretches from the Euphrates river in Syria to the northern parts of India, and is a threat to the Roman Empire.
● 53 BC: Parthian cavalry defeat a force of Roman infantry at Carrhae (Turkey).

● Early Egyptian farmers (above) using oxen and a plow.

● 1570 BC: the "New Kingdom" begins in Egypt. The empire expands as far as Syria and the southern lands of Sudan.

● Egypt is weakened by the increasing power of the Amun, the priests of the sun god Re. This slows down economic and political development. Foreigners from Libya settle in Egypt and establish a dynasty of nine pharaohs.
● c.814 BC: the Phoenicians establish the city of Carthage.

● Egypt for the next 700 years (730–30 BC) is mostly ruled by invaders: Nubians, Persians, Macedonians and Greeks.

● Evidence of the use of iron in Africa south of the Sahara desert, c.500 BC, and of ironworking in Nigeria, c.450 BC.

● c.196 BC: in Egypt the Rosetta stone is written in Greek, Egyptian hieroglyphics and Demotic (a late form of Egyptian language).
● 30 BC: Cleopatra VII commits suicide, as Egypt falls to the Romans. Egypt now becomes a province of the Roman Empire.

● The cities of Harappa and Mohenjo-Daro (below) are built in the Indus Valley. The civilization survives until c.1700 BC.

● The Shang (c.1750–1050 BC), China's first dynasty, uses bronze (above), unlike the earlier Longshan and Yangshao cultures.

● In China the Zhou dynasty follows the Shang in 1050 BC. In 770 BC the Eastern Zhou era begins.

● Gautama Siddhartha, founder of Buddhism, is born in India c.563 BC.
● Confucius, the famous Chinese philosopher, is born in 551 BC.
● In northern India the Aryans have about 16 kingdoms, including Magadha. Hinduism and the caste system are established by 500 BC.

● 483 BC: the Buddha dies. The Great Stupa in Sanchi, India, (below) contained parts of the Buddha's body.

● The Mauryan Empire in India breaks up after King Ashoka's death in 238 BC.
● In China the Qin dynasty begins in 221 BC.

● Settlements in Meso-america grow their food.
● The highland villagers of Mexico make coiled pottery.

● A head portrait in stone of an Olmec ruler (above), from Mesoamerica.

● In Mesoamerica La Venta is now the major Olmec site.

● Hieroglyphic inscriptions are drawn at the Zapotec settlement at Monte Alban (c.500 BC). They are the earliest example of writing in the Americas.
● The Chavin culture of Peru continues to influence the Andean region through its religious beliefs.
● In southern Peru the Paracas culture develops.

● The Nazca people have emerged as the dominant culture on the south coast of Peru. They carve shapes in the desert.

● The Hopewell culture, second of the three eastern North American prehistoric cultures, is well established.

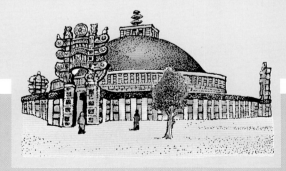

11

CITIES AND EMPIRES OF MESOPOTAMIA

THE WORLD'S FIRST cities grew up in Mesopotamia. They developed from the villages in the flat land between the rivers Tigris and Euphrates, an area called Mesopotamia. Sumer, in southern Mesopotamia, had such fertile soil and produced so much food that the villages there gradually grew in size. By about 4000 BC these villages had become cities, each having a population of several thousand. Each was surrounded by a wall and dominated by a large temple. The cities' people had different jobs – there were craftspeople, soldiers, farmers and priests, for example. The civilization of Mesopotamia's cities lasted for over 3,500 years. For over 1,500 years Mesopotamia was divided into city-states. Each city, and the land around it, had its own king. These city-states traded with each other but they fought each other as well. Sometimes the ruler of one city managed to conquer a large area and so founded an empire.

Marshes of southern Mesopotamia
Mesopotamia had few natural advantages apart from river water and soil, so its people often had to bring in important materials such as hardwood and metals from other places. On these marshlands, near the Persian Gulf, however, the people of southern Mesopotamia found fish, birds and reeds. They used reeds for making mats and writing implements.

The ziggurat of Ur
The ziggurat was built in about 2000 BC. Ziggurats were religious buildings which were built next to temples in Mesopotamian cities. On top of the ziggurat was a small temple. Each city worshiped its own god or goddess for its protection. For example, the city of Ur worshiped the Moon god Nanna.

The first writing
The invention of writing in about 3000 BC was one of Mesopotamia's great achievements. The earliest writing (right) was made up of simple drawings of objects, called pictograms. Later the pictograms were made even simpler and were used to represent the sounds of speech. Kings used scribes (far right) to write down their laws.

The pillar of law
Mesopotamian kings made laws to help keep order in their cities and empires. This pillar (6½ feet high) shows 282 laws made by King Hammurabi of Babylon. It would have been written by a scribe. The king is at the top, standing before the Sun god Shamash.

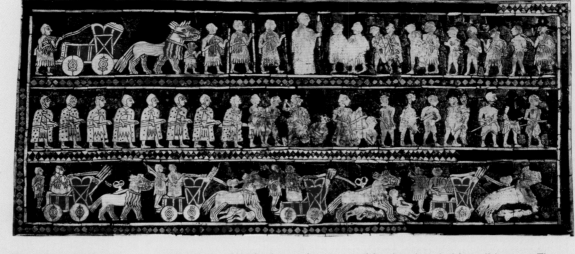

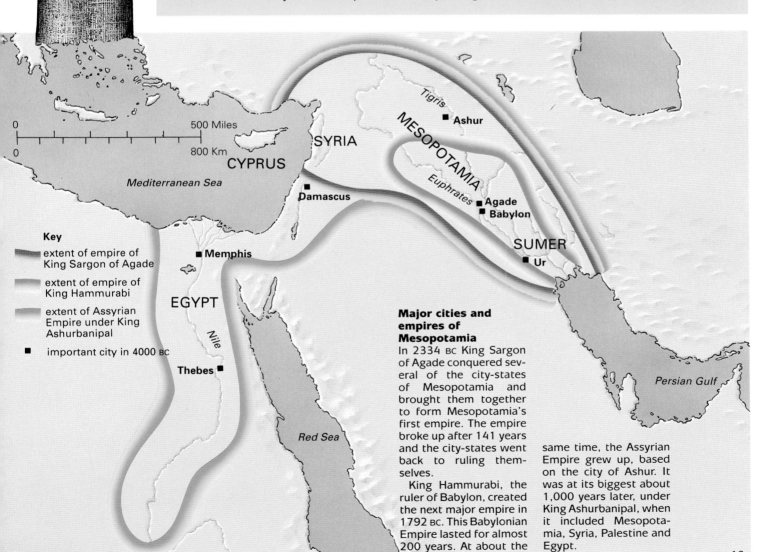

The army of King Ur
Some of the richest objects from the civilization of ancient Mesopotamia were discovered at the site of the city of Ur. This mosaic panel appears on a box which was discovered in a royal cemetery at Ur. It is 4,000 years old and is made with shell, red limestone and a semi-precious stone called lapis lazuli. It shows a king and his victorious army after a battle. In the top line, enemy prisoners with hands tied are brought before the king, who is shown standing in the center. In the middle line is a column of the king's soldiers. In the bottom line are the king's battle wagons, which are pulled by wild asses. There were as many as 10,000 men in some Mesopotamian armies. The other side of the box is also decorated. It shows the king and his followers having a feast to celebrate their victory.

Key

- extent of empire of King Sargon of Agade
- extent of empire of King Hammurabi
- extent of Assyrian Empire under King Ashurbanipal
- ■ important city in 4000 BC

Major cities and empires of Mesopotamia
In 2334 BC King Sargon of Agade conquered several of the city-states of Mesopotamia and brought them together to form Mesopotamia's first empire. The empire broke up after 141 years and the city-states went back to ruling themselves.

King Hammurabi, the ruler of Babylon, created the next major empire in 1792 BC. This Babylonian Empire lasted for almost 200 years. At about the same time, the Assyrian Empire grew up, based on the city of Ashur. It was at its biggest about 1,000 years later, under King Ashurbanipal, when it included Mesopotamia, Syria, Palestine and Egypt.

13

ANCIENT EGYPT

THE CIVILIZATION OF Ancient Egypt, like that of Mesopotamia, grew up in fertile land by a river. Egypt's river is the River Nile. Unlike Mesopotamia, though, Ancient Egypt was a single kingdom for most of its existence, ruled by a pharaoh, or king. At first there were two separate kingdoms, Lower Egypt at the mouth of the Nile, and Upper Egypt in the south. But in about 3100 BC, Menes, the pharaoh of Upper Egypt, added Lower Egypt to his kingdom. He built a capital city at Memphis. All the fertile land and minerals of the area were then controlled by him, which made him very powerful.

The civilization of Ancient Egypt lasted for over 3,500 years. One reason it survived so long was its location: it was surrounded by deserts, which protected it from attack. Another reason was that Egypt's pharaohs used very skilled and educated people to run the country.

The River Nile
Ancient Egypt was a wealthy country, even though most of the land was desert. This was because Egypt also had fertile soil – found in a narrow strip along the River Nile. Every year in August and September the Nile flooded because of rainfall far to the south. This left the land around it moist and fertile for growing crops.

The pyramids and Sphinx at Giza
The Ancient Egyptians believed that after death a person's soul went on to enjoy an eternal life in the kingdom of the god Osiris. They imagined this kingdom to be like a perfect Egypt. They built pyramids as tombs for the dead pharaohs and buried with them the things they might need for this afterlife. They believed that if people were important on earth, then they would also be important in their lives after death. The early pharaohs even had living people buried with them.

The most magnificent pyramids are at Giza. Also at Giza is the Great Sphinx. It shows King Kheperen (2520 BC– 2494 BC) as a man-lion protecting his country.

14

Egyptian mummies
The Egyptians believed that life continued after death, and that the dead body had to be preserved to house the body's spirit. The best results were achieved by first drying out the body. The brain was then removed by pulling it out of the nose with hooks, and all the body's insides were also removed. The body was then packed with linen to give back its shape. A mask was placed over the head and the whole body was wrapped with bandages (see above). The word "mummy" comes from the Arabic for bitumen, "mumiya." At one time people wrongly thought that bitumen, a tarlike substance, was used in the preservation of the bodies.

Hunting in marshland
People in Ancient Egypt were divided into groups, in order of importance. At the top was the pharaoh, or king. Below him came the senior priests, officials, noblemen and army commanders. In this scene from a tomb painting, a nobleman and his family are hunting birds in the marshes. His wife is shown as much smaller than he is to indicate that she is less important, but women were allowed to own their own property and land. Noble families had servants, who were Egyptians, and slaves, who were often foreigners. Most ordinary Egyptians were farmers.

Cattle taxes and hieroglyphics
Every year noblemen inspected and counted their cattle and then gave some of them to the pharaoh as taxes. This wall painting of cattle being inspected was found inside a tomb. It also shows Ancient Egyptian writing, called hieroglyphics. This was a form of picture-writing.

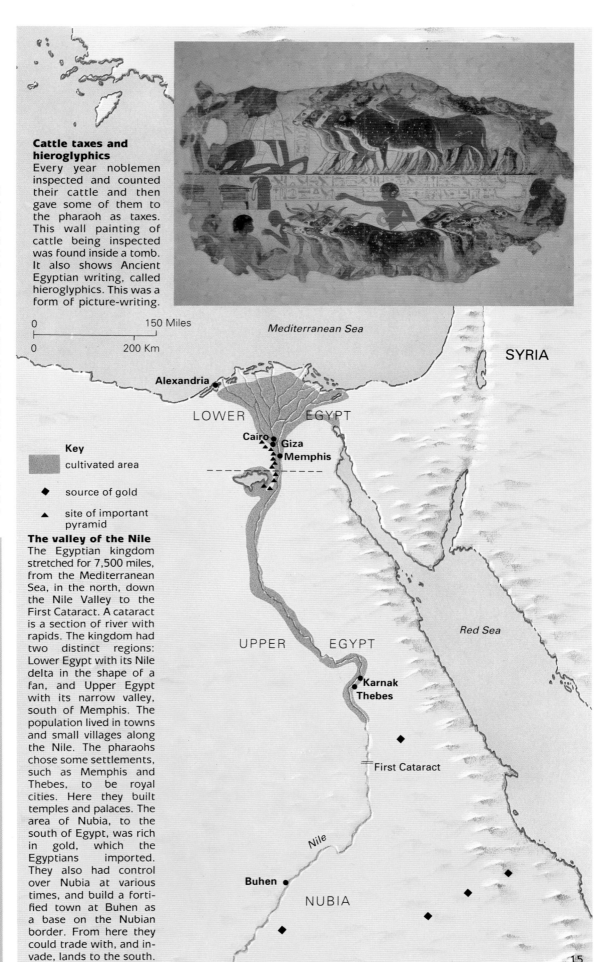

Key

cultivated area

◆ source of gold

▲ site of important pyramid

The valley of the Nile
The Egyptian kingdom stretched for 7,500 miles, from the Mediterranean Sea, in the north, down the Nile Valley to the First Cataract. A cataract is a section of river with rapids. The kingdom had two distinct regions: Lower Egypt with its Nile delta in the shape of a fan, and Upper Egypt with its narrow valley, south of Memphis. The population lived in towns and small villages along the Nile. The pharaohs chose some settlements, such as Memphis and Thebes, to be royal cities. Here they built temples and palaces. The area of Nubia, to the south of Egypt, was rich in gold, which the Egyptians imported. They also had control over Nubia at various times, and build a fortified town at Buhen as a base on the Nubian border. From here they could trade with, and invade, lands to the south.

15

INDIAN CIVILIZATIONS

THE THIRD ANCIENT civilization to develop in a fertile valley emerged along the Indus River in about 2500 BC. This is where Pakistan and northwest India are today. Very little is known about the Indus Valley civilization, since we cannot understand their writing, and no tombs have been found. The major cities were Mohenjo-Daro and Harappa, and most people lived as farmers.

The Indus Valley civilization lasted only 800 years, until about 1700 BC. This is much shorter than those of Mesopotamia and Egypt. It is possible that the soil was no longer fertile enough to feed the population, which then moved away. It may also have been linked to the arrival of a new group of people in the area. From about 1500 BC the Aryans moved southward from the area of modern Iran into northwest India. They set up kingdoms all over northern India. Eventually one of these, called Magadha, grew more powerful than the others. Its rulers created the Mauryan Empire in about 300 BC.

Indus Valley seals
We know that the Indus Valley people were skilled and could write because we have found their stone seals. Several thousand still exist, each about ¾ inch square. They were used to stamp property, showing ownership of goods. Most of the seals have an image on them – such as this bull – and signs in the Indus script. Indus writing is based on picture symbols. We know of almost 400 such symbols, but we do not yet understand what they mean.

Rulers of the Indus Valley civilization
It is possible that the rulers of the Indus Valley were priest-kings. This sculpture provides an important piece of evidence. The decoration on the man's robe was also used in Mesopotamia and Egypt as a religious symbol.

The main cities of the Indus Valley civilizations must have had rulers. Each of these cities had a citadel, or fortress, built on top of a specially built mound. It is likely that the citadel was meant for the use of a ruler or rulers. In one of these citadels a large bathtub used for religious ceremonies was discovered, and this provides more evidence for the idea of priest-king rulers. Below the citadels lay the rest of the city, which covered a large area. Cities such as Mohenjo-Daro were built according to a plan. The wide streets formed a grid pattern.

At both Mohenjo-Daro and Harappa there were large granaries for storing grain. The surrounding villages may have paid this grain as a tax.

Indus Valley games
The Indus Valley people were keen game players. Dice, playing pieces and bases from board games have been found in the ruins of the cities. Children's toys have also been found. They include small terracotta (baked clay) animals and models of ox-drawn carts.

Buddhism

Buddhism, like Hinduism, came from ancient India. Many people disliked the way Hindu society divided people into groups. Among them was Gautama Siddhartha (563-483 BC). He turned his back on his life as a wealthy prince to search for wisdom. After six years of wandering he found it through a process of deep thinking, called meditation. The picture shows the Buddha meditating. This allowed him to overcome human weaknesses, including greed and anger. He became the Buddha, the "Enlightened One," and carried his message around northeast India.

Hinduism

Hinduism is the main religion of India. It is also, along with Judaism, the world's oldest surviving religion. It began when Aryan immigrants were spreading across northern India. At first the Aryans and the native Indians worshiped different gods, but by 800 BC their beliefs had blended together. The Aryans did not mix with the Indians because they believed the Indians came from a lower group of society. All Hindus worship the chief gods: Brahma, Vishnu and Shiva; and they believe in reincarnation. This is the belief that the soul of a dead person comes back to life in a different body after their death. This new body can be that of another human or an animal, depending on how well the person has lived his or her life.

There are many different groups within Hinduism who worship other gods as well as the chief gods. One of these, a goddess, is shown in this terracotta plaque. Some of these gods or goddesses are worshiped only in a local area.

Hindu society has four main social groups or castes into which every Hindu is born. The castes that are considered most pure are the priests, followed by warriors and nobles. Next come farmers and traders and, after them, laborers and servants. The caste system started over 2,000 years ago. Later a fifth caste was added – the "untouchables." They are considered to be the lowest group and are allowed to do only the dirtiest jobs.

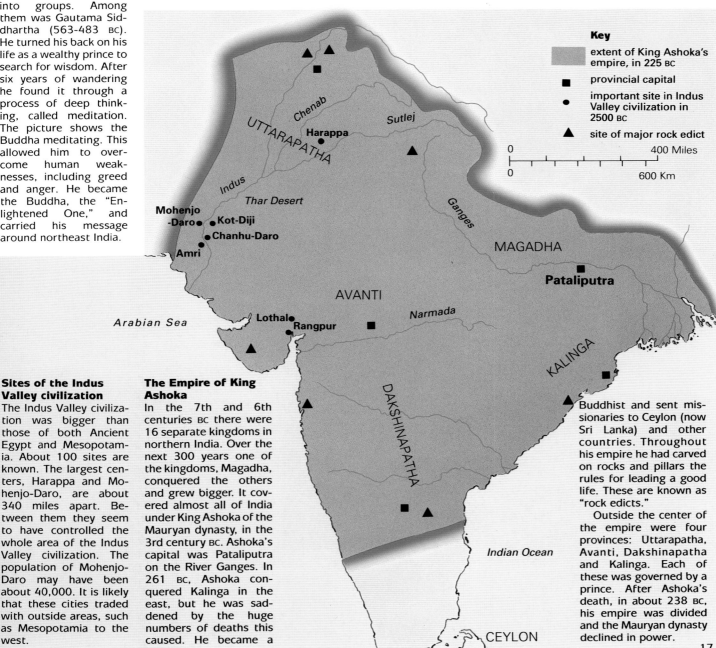

Key

- extent of King Ashoka's empire, in 225 BC
- ■ provincial capital
- ● important site in Indus Valley civilization in 2500 BC
- ▲ site of major rock edict

| 0 | | 400 Miles |
| 0 | | 600 Km |

Sites of the Indus Valley civilization

The Indus Valley civilization was bigger than those of both Ancient Egypt and Mesopotamia. About 100 sites are known. The largest centers, Harappa and Mohenjo-Daro, are about 340 miles apart. Between them they seem to have controlled the whole area of the Indus Valley civilization. The population of Mohenjo-Daro may have been about 40,000. It is likely that these cities traded with outside areas, such as Mesopotamia to the west.

The Empire of King Ashoka

In the 7th and 6th centuries BC there were 16 separate kingdoms in northern India. Over the next 300 years one of the kingdoms, Magadha, conquered the others and grew bigger. It covered almost all of India under King Ashoka of the Mauryan dynasty, in the 3rd century BC. Ashoka's capital was Pataliputra on the River Ganges. In 261 BC, Ashoka conquered Kalinga in the east, but he was saddened by the huge numbers of deaths this caused. He became a Buddhist and sent missionaries to Ceylon (now Sri Lanka) and other countries. Throughout his empire he had carved on rocks and pillars the rules for leading a good life. These are known as "rock edicts."

Outside the center of the empire were four provinces: Uttarapatha, Avanti, Dakshinapatha and Kalinga. Each of these was governed by a prince. After Ashoka's death, in about 238 BC, his empire was divided and the Mauryan dynasty declined in power.

17

CIVILIZATIONS IN EARLY CHINA

THE WORLD'S FIRST three early civilizations – Mesopotamia, Ancient Egypt and the Indus Valley – were all eventually replaced by new cultures. The fourth civilization, that of China, continues today.

In about 1750 BC a kingdom appeared in north China, in the middle reaches of the Yellow River. It was ruled by kings of the Shang dynasty, or line of rulers. The Shang kingdom used writing (the first Chinese script), a calendar and money. It lasted for almost 1,000 years but then broke up into many smaller kingdoms and city-states, which fought each other. In 221 BC, Shi Huangdi of Qin took control of northern and central China to become the first emperor of China. Qin is pronounced "chin" in Chinese, and it is where the name China comes from. The Qin dynasty did not last for very long. It ended with the death of Shi Huangdi in 210 BC, and was followed by the Han and Western Jin dynasties over the next 500 years, until AD 311.

Chinese bronze-working
One of the most skilled crafts in early China was making objects from bronze. Kings and nobles ordered the production of many bronze vessels, made from molten metal poured into molds. Most, such as this animal-shaped bowl, were used for offering sacrifices to ancestors. Vessels were often buried with their owners.

China's Yellow River
The valleys of the Yellow River, where Chinese civilization began, have a fine sandy soil called loess. Loess is easy to farm and fertile enough to produce large crops of cereals, such as millet, to feed a large population. One of these valleys is the Wei He valley, seen here. The river carries huge quantities of loess and was named for the color created by the soil. It is also called China's Sorrow because its many floods have brought death and hunger to local people.

Oracle bone
People in early China believed that the souls of the dead went to heaven. The souls of dead kings and nobles could then appeal to the gods to benefit those still alive. So kings and nobles, during their lives, made sacrifices of food and drink to get their ancestors to plead for them in heaven. Ancestors were also asked about important events such as the chances of winning a war. Oracle bones, usually the bones of a cow or ox, were used for this. A bone was heated until it cracked. The cracks were interpreted and the answer then written on the bone.

Chinese money

The Chinese were possibly the first people to use money for buying and selling goods. They used polished cowrie shells as money. Cowries are small sea creatures. 700 cowries were found in a royal tomb from the 12th century BC. Later, the Chinese made coins in the shape of cowrie shells. During the years when there was much fighting in China (428-221 BC), rulers in eastern China made bronze coins shaped like daggers. Other rulers made spade-shaped coins.

The first emperor's terracotta army

In 221 BC, Shi Huangdi united north and central China. In 1974 astonishing evidence of his power was discovered. People digging a well close to his tomb, near Xi'an in northwest China, found an enormous pit. In it was a life-size model army of over 6,000 hollow soldiers, horses and chariots, made of terracotta (baked clay). They were buried with the emperor to "guard" him from danger. The soldiers were all in military formation and originally carried weapons. The weapons, though, were missing when they found the tomb, and were probably stolen when a rebel general destroyed the tomb only four years after the emperor's

death. Each terracotta figure was modeled and painted separately and each had a different face, so thousands of craftsmen and workers must have worked on them. From these figures we have discovered a great deal about the armor, formation and uniforms of the imperial army of early China. The actual tomb of the emperor has not yet been excavated, and more wonderful discoveries are expected.

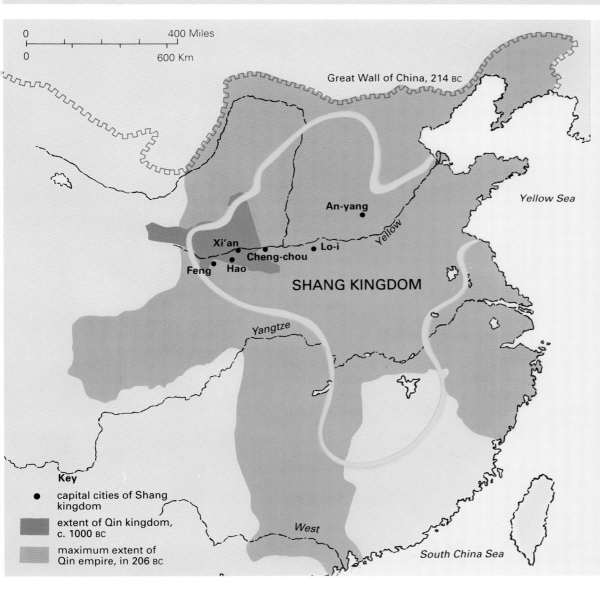

0 |—————| 400 Miles
0 |—————| 600 Km

Great Wall of China, 214 BC

Yellow Sea

An-yang

Xi'an
Cheng-chou • Lo-i
Feng • Hao

Yellow

SHANG KINGDOM

Yangtze

West

South China Sea

Key

● capital cities of Shang kingdom

extent of Qin kingdom, c. 1000 BC

maximum extent of Qin empire, in 206 BC

Early China and the Qin Empire

The first Chinese state, the Shang kingdom, was in north China. Its capital cities stood on the north China plain, at the foot of mountains. From there the Shang kings could control both the important mineral sources, such as metals, in the mountains, and the agricultural villages on the plain. Shang Chinese culture gradually spread to the Yangtze River in the south. This larger area was first ruled by Shi Huangdi. He ruled with armies and officials. He organized huge numbers of laborers to work for him. Important roads were built, and earth walls were joined together to form one "Great Wall" along the northern frontier to keep out the enemies of the empire. The original Great Wall was completed during the Qin dynasty, in about 214 BC, and stretched for about 1,400 miles.

19

THE PERSIAN EMPIRE

THERE HAD BEEN great empires in the Middle East from 2334 BC, such as the Babylonian and Assyrian empires, but the biggest was the Persian Empire. It was begun by Cyrus the Great, king of Persia from about 559 BC to 529 BC.

Good government and communications were needed to rule such a large empire. Darius I (522–486 BC) provided these. The early Persian rulers such as Cyrus and Darius I followed a sensible policy of allowing the local peoples of the empire to keep their religions and customs. This encouraged them to accept the king's rule. Cyrus, for example, allowed the Jews to return to their holy city of Jerusalem, 50 years after the Babylonians had forced them to leave. Both Darius and his successor, Xerxes (486–465 BC), tried to take over Greece, but they were defeated. The last Persian ruler, Darius III (about 336–330 BC) was defeated by Alexander the Great of Macedonia in 331 BC.

Ruins of Persepolis
Some of the Persian kings celebrated their victories, wealth and power by building large palaces. Darius used the old city of Susa as his capital, but in 520 BC he also founded a second capital and palace at Persepolis, and impressive ruins of this city still exist. Persepolis took nearly 50 years to build, and people from many different parts of the empire were involved in its construction. As a result, a variety of architectural styles can be seen there. The buildings include audience halls and reception rooms, storerooms for tributes and other valuables, and military quarters. The tallest building is the "apadana," an immense hall containing 36 columns measuring nearly 65 feet in height. The kings of Persepolis used the hall to welcome and impress visitors.

The Oxus treasure
The kings and nobles of the Persian Empire enjoyed owning valuable objects. The Oxus treasure shows just how wealthy they were, and the great skill of the Persian craftsmen. It is made up of about 170 gold and silver objects and about 1,500 coins. It was found near the Oxus River in the northeast corner of the empire.

The Royal messenger
Under Darius I, a network of roads was built to link Persia and the royal court to the other parts of the empire. The most important of these was the Royal Road, which ran from Susa in Persia to Sardis in Anatolia (now Turkey). Messengers used these roads, carrying letters from one area to another.

Tribute bearers

This sculpture (below) from the king's palace at Persepolis shows the payment of tributes to the royal court. This happened once a year, at New Year. Tributes were taxes paid in goods. Different regions, or "satrapies," paid with different goods. For example, Egypt sent bulls and textiles such as linen, and Bactria sent camels and vessels. The kings were proud they had power to get these different areas to pay their tributes, and so had scenes like these depicted on the sculptures in their palaces.

Tombs of the Persian kings

Darius I was buried in a sacred place near Persepolis. He had a tomb cut into a cliff. The front of the tomb (right) is in the shape of a cross. The central part was made to look like the front of a royal palace. Above this is a sculpture of Darius praying to his god. He stands on a block of stone supported by figures representing the 30 peoples of the empire. Inside there is a room, and behind it are spaces for nine coffins. Three later kings have tombs like this in the same sacred place.

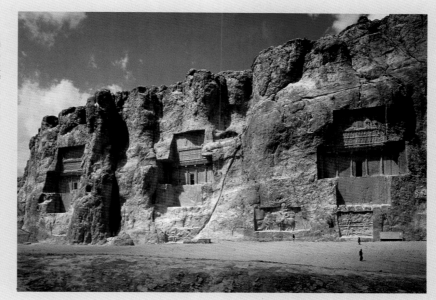

Key

extent of the Persian Empire under King Darius I

tribute paid by the regions of the empire:

○ horses
● camels
● cloth
● vessels
● weapons

═══ route of the Royal Road

| 0 | | 600 Miles |
| 0 | | 1,000 Km |

The Persian Empire under Darius I

Cyrus the Great took only 30 years to expand the Persian Empire so that it covered the whole of Mesopotamia, Anatolia (now Turkey), the eastern Mediterranean, and the areas of modern Pakistan and Afghanistan. The Persian Empire then stretched for 2,800 miles from north Africa and the Black Sea in the west to the Indus Valley in the east. It was very difficult to rule such a vast area because of the many different peoples and cultures. Darius I divided the empire into provinces called "satrapies." Each satrapy was controlled by a local ruler or satrap. The satrap's job was to look after the roads, collect the tribute and find men to serve in the empire's army. Most satraps were Persians.

Governing the empire was also made easier by the road network. The roads were also used for trade, in raw materials, carpets and spices. Darius I made trade more efficient by providing a gold coinage and by building a canal between the River Nile and the Red Sea.

GREEK CIVILIZATIONS

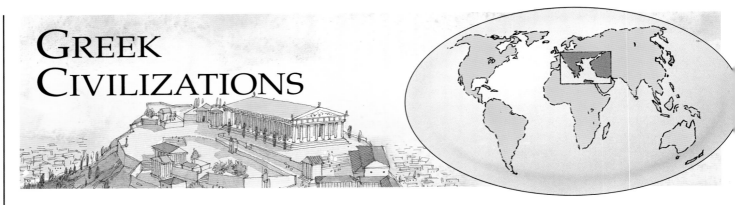

THE THREE EARLIEST civilizations in Europe all began in the area of modern Greece. The first is called Minoan. It flowered on Crete and some Aegean islands from 1900 to 1400 BC. Little was known about the Minoans until the ruins of their impressive palace at Knossos were excavated in the 20th century. However, historians still cannot translate their script. The second civilization, called Mycenaean, prospered on mainland Greece from 1550 BC to about 1150 BC. Their script was decoded in 1952. We have learned that the Mycenaeans worshiped many of the gods which appear in later Greek religion. The third of the early Greek civilizations was that of "Classical" Greece. It began in the 8th century BC on the Greek mainland, when city-states developed on the plains between the mountains. Each city-state had its own rulers, government and laws. The most important city-states of Classical Greece were Sparta and Athens. Athens developed a form of government called democracy, in which the citizens had some influence over how the state would be ruled.

A Mycenaean mask
Like the Minoan civilization, the Mycenaean civilization was made up of small kingdoms. It was dominated by the kingdom of Mycenae. Their kings were rich because they controlled the trade of valuable metals between Europe and the Middle East. The earliest of the kings were buried in deep pits with splendid treasures, such as this solid gold mask.

Hoplite soldier
The Classical Greeks were among the best soldiers in the ancient world. Their armies did not depend on chariots and cavalry, but on the foot soldier, or "hoplite." Hoplites had very good armor: a metal helmet, a breastplate and shin guards. Each hoplite also carried a shield and long spear. The hoplites fought in lines, advancing against the enemy packed together, with their shields held in front.

The Minoans at Knossos
Minoan civilization was named after the legendary king of Crete, Minos. The island of Crete was the center of the civilization. It was divided into small kingdoms, each with its own city, and ruled from a palace. Knossos was the largest city, with a population of about 100,000 and a magnificent palace (above). Here there were royal apartments for the king and queen, workshops, storerooms and schoolrooms. Outside the palace grounds there were smaller town houses.

Most of the Minoan people lived in the countryside as farmers. They kept animals and grew crops such as wheat, olives and grapes. Wall paintings at Knossos also show that they fished and hunted. The Minoans also traded with foreign countries. Their pots have been found in lands around the eastern Mediterranean, so they must have had a good fleet of ships.

Socrates, a Greek thinker

Athens was a center for philosophers in the 5th and 4th centuries BC. The best known of these were Socrates (469-399 BC), Plato (429-347 BC) and later Aristotle (384-322 BC). Socrates lived a colorful life and had been a soldier as well as a philosopher. He was a very skillful debater, and often made the person arguing against him appear to be a fool. When he did this to important politicians in Athens they became angry. They got their revenge by accusing him of not worshiping the city's gods. After a dramatic trial Socrates was condemned to death, and forced to drink poison.

The round temple at Delphi

The Greeks worshiped many gods and goddesses, who they believed could influence events in the human world. Before beginning an important project, they would seek advice from an oracle, a special site where a priest or priestess would speak on behalf of a god. The most famous oracle was at Delphi. Here the priestess explained the views of the god Apollo.

During the Persian invasion of Greece the Athenians consulted the oracle at Delphi.

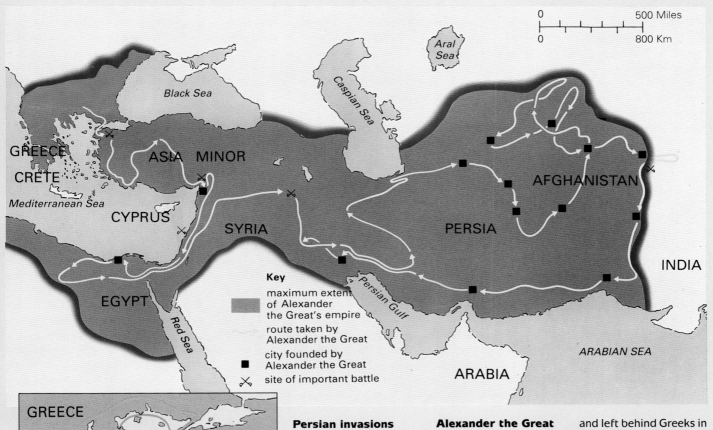

Key
maximum extent of Alexander the Great's empire
route taken by Alexander the Great
■ city founded by Alexander the Great
⚔ site of important battle

GREECE
ASIA MINOR
Thermopylae
Delphi
Salamis
Marathon
Athens
Mediterranean Sea

Key
route of Persian invasion in 490 BC
route of Persian invasion in 480 BC
⚔ site of important battle
0 ____ 100 Miles
0 ____ 200 Km

Persian invasions

In 490 BC King Darius I invaded Greece. His ships landed at Marathon. Despite the size of his army, Darius' men were defeated by the superior Greek hoplite army. In 480 BC the next Persian king, Xerxes, tried again. The opposing armies met on a narrow mountain pass at Thermopylae. Helped by a Greek traitor, the Persians found a way through the pass, and were able to surround and kill the Greek king, Leonidas.

Alexander the Great and Persia

Alexander became king of Macedonia in Greece in 336 BC. He was a great military leader, and over the next 13 years conquered a vast empire to the east of Greece. This is why he was called Alexander the Great. In 334 BC he invaded the Persian Empire, and he gradually worked his way through Asia Minor, Egypt, Syria, Persia (now Iran) and Afghanistan. Alexander founded many cities in his new empire, and left behind Greeks in each area. This meant that the Greek language and culture reached an enormous area. He also tried to include local people in the running of the empire, because he could see that it was far too big to be run from Greece.

Alexander died of a fever in 323 BC, at the age of 32. Only someone as powerful as he was could hold his empire together, and so, over the next 25 years, it broke up.

23

THE ROMAN EMPIRE

ONE OF THE strongest empires in history was created by people who came from the city of Rome, in Italy. Cities had first appeared in Mesopotamia (see page 12) and then in other places in the Middle East. From about 800 BC the people of central Italy also began to create cities. From about 300 BC, Rome grew to become more powerful than the other cities of Italy. Between 334 BC and 264 BC, the Romans conquered all of Italy, and Rome became the leading city on the northern side of the Mediterranean Sea.

On the southern side, the leading city was Carthage, which controlled lands in Africa and Spain. Rome and Carthage fought three wars, each wanting to dominate the Mediterranean. Rome won all three, and completely destroyed Carthage in 146 BC. Over the next 250 years Roman territory continued to expand into a vast Mediterranean empire.

An aqueduct in Spain The Romans built impressive bridges, or aqueducts, to carry water in pipes. This one leads to the city of Segovia in Spain, from a source about 10 miles away. Arches were an important feature in Roman construction.

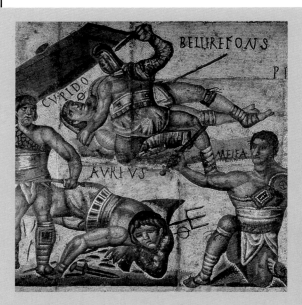

At the baths
The Romans liked to keep their bodies clean and fit. They built elaborate public baths throughout the empire. After undressing, the visitor could exercise and then sit in a warm room. Next came the sweat room, where oil was rubbed into the body to loosen the dirt. This was then scraped off with a strigil, a scraper rather like a blunt comb. Finally came a plunge into a cold bath. Roman toilets were very public and large, seating as many as thirty men and women in the open.

Atlantic Ocean

Sego

A Roman mosaic
Pictures of Roman life can be seen in the mosaic floors which survive from their houses and palaces. A mosaic was made by laying thousands of small stones or glass tiles to form a pattern, set in a bed of fine mortar. This scene from a mosaic shows a contest between gladiators. Gladiators were specially trained to fight each other at organized contests. These took place in a public arena for the entertainment of the townspeople.

Hannibal's elephants
Hannibal was a general who led the army of Carthage into Italy to fight against Rome. He took his army and 38 elephants across the Alps.

The first emperor
For almost 500 years Rome was ruled by two elected leaders, called consuls. After a period of civil war and confusion, Augustus (27 BC-AD 14) made himself emperor with total power.

Pompeii and Vesuvius
In AD 79 a volcano near Naples, called Mount Vesuvius, erupted. Hot stones and ash burst out of it, smothering the countryside and the nearby town of Pompeii. As a result at least 2,000 people were killed.

The town was discovered again in 1748. It shows us how Roman towns were planned. Straight streets crossed the town, forming a grid pattern. In the town center was an open area, called the forum, which was surrounded by a hall, offices, law courts and shops.

The extent of the Roman Empire
In AD 114 the empire reached its greatest size, under Emperor Trajan (AD 98-117). It covered over 2,500 miles from west to east and had about 60 million inhabitants. The Romans tried to use natural frontiers such as rivers or mountain ranges to mark the borders of their empire. Otherwise, they built their own fortified frontiers such as Hadrian's Wall in Britain. They divided the empire into provinces, run by governors. Latin was the language for all officials and they applied the Roman system of laws. Some people in the empire became Roman citizens.

However, fierce tribes such as the Goths and Vandals from outside the empire began to attack it. The empire had been split in 285 into an eastern and western empire. The Western Empire finally collapsed in 476, but the Eastern Empire lasted another thousand years, and became known as the Byzantine Empire.

0	500 Miles
0	800 Km

Key
• the Roman names for cities are given in brackets
— extent of the Roman Empire in A.D. 117

York (Eboracum)
BRITAIN
London (Londinium)
GERMANY
Loire
Rhine
Danube
FRANCE
Black Sea
SPAIN
Nimes (Nemausus)
ITALY
CORSICA
Rome
Byzantium (Constantinople)
Thessalonica
SARDINIA
Pompeii
GREECE
Athens (Athenae)
Antioch (Antiochia)
SICILY
CYPRUS
Carthage (Carthago)
AFRICA
CRETE
Mediterranean Sea
EGYPT
Nile

25

THE MIDDLE AGES

The decline of the Roman Empire, and rise of the Ottomans.
Rich cultures flourish in Africa, the Americas and the Far East.

EUROPE

● 79: in southern Italy the cities of Pompeii and Herculaneum are destroyed by the eruption of the volcano Vesuvius. At least 2,000 people are killed.
● The Roman Empire reaches its greatest extent under Emperor Trajan (98–117), but in the 3rd century it faces barbarian invasions from Goths of northern Europe, and civil war as rival generals squabble for power.

● 295: The Roman Empire is split in two. The goddess of fortune (below) represents the capital of the Eastern Empire, Constantinople.

● From the 7th century onward the Eastern Roman Empire (called the Byzantine Empire) is frequently at war against the Slavs and Arabs.
● Emperor Justinian (527–65) recovers some of the lost lands of the Western Empire, in southern Spain, North Africa and Italy. But these are soon lost again after Justinian's death.

● Charlemagne creates a huge empire in Europe and forces the Saxons to accept Christianity. In 800 the Pope crowns him Holy Roman Emperor.

THE MIDDLE EAST

● 132: the Jewish rebellion against Rome fails, and so the Jewish people begin to move out of Palestine. This is known as the diaspora.

● Rome is at war with the Sassanian dynasty of Persia and surrenders Mesopotamia. The river Tigris is the boundary between them.

● 643: the Sassanian Empire, which reaches its greatest extent c.579, is overthrown by Arabs.
● Islam is founded in the 7th century in Arabia.

● The Islamic empire of the Abbasids flourishes, lasting until 1258. An Abbasid caliph builds the Great Mosque of Samarra (Iraq) (above).

AFRICA

● Rome replaces Egypt as the dominant power in North Africa. This Egyptian statue of Anubis, jackal-headed god of embalming, is wearing a Roman toga (above).

● Christianity arrives in Africa in the 4th century.
● c.320: King Ezana of Axum, in the northeast, is converted to Christianity.
● The people of Axum build the 98-foot-high obelisks which are to make their town famous. Axum is the most powerful maritime trading state on the Red Sea.
● The nearby Kingdom of Meroe declines.

● Islam spreads from Arabia to Egypt, and Egypt becomes a Muslim state in 641.
● 670: the Friday mosque is founded in Tunisia (above).

● Early Arab settlements appear along the east coast.
● Toward the end of the period, the city of Cairo is founded in Egypt.

ASIA AND AUSTRALASIA

● This bronze chariot (below) is made during the Han dynasty.
● 220: the last Han emperor hands over power as the country splits into three rival kingdoms.

● Northern India reaches its greatest phase under the Guptas of Magadha. The dynasty lasts 200 years and Buddhism becomes popular.

● Buddhism expands further. Japan adopts it as the official religion in 594, and China adopts it in 624 under the new Tang dynasty.

● 8th century: this elephant wall (above) is built around a stupa in Ceylon.
● 907: the Tang dynasty of China has disintegrated.

NORTH AND SOUTH AMERICA

● The foundations for the city of Teotihuacán are laid, including the largest artificial structure of pre-Columbian America: the Pyramid of the Sun.

● Teotihuacán reaches its peak, with a population of 200,000.
● The Mayan civilization develops in Central America, with stone-built cities at Tikal and Palenque.

● The Mayan city at Copán (above).
● Early 8th century: the first real North American towns, known as the Temple Mound culture, appear in the Mississippi Valley.

● c.750: Teotihuacán is destroyed by fire, but it continues to attract pilgrims.
● The Mayan civilization is in decline in the south, but new centers develop in the north. Later, the Toltecs rebuild the abandoned Mayan city of Chichén Itzá.
● c.800: in Peru, the fortified city of Huari is suddenly abandoned.

In Europe the Roman Empire reaches its peak, and by 500 is in decline. The Christianity it helped to spread is challenged by the impact of Islam from the 7th century onward. In the 14th century Europe is devastated by the Black Death, a plague which kills up to 25 million people.

In Central Africa cultures develop independently of European influences, and the riches of these kingdoms are reported by Arab traders to Europeans. The wealth and power of China continues to dominate the Far East.

In Central America, the culture of the Mayan civilization blossoms from c.300, but has faded by the 10th century. In its place emerges that of the Toltecs. In North America the first towns develop in the 8th century.

● 1066: William I of Normandy invades England. The Normans build many castles (below).
● 1096: the First Crusade.

● King Henry II of England rules over Anjou, Aquitaine, Normandy, Gascony, and Brittany in the Angevin Empire.

● 1204: King John of England loses French lands.
● 1241: the German towns of Hamburg and Lübeck set up a trading association, which leads to the formation of the Hanseatic League. By 1400 150 towns and cities are members, and it controls trade in the North and Baltic Seas.

● 1337–1453: the Hundred Years War between England and France, over English lands in France.
● 1347–53: the Black Death, a plague carried from Asia by fleas on rats and humans, spreads across Europe, killing up to a quarter of the population.

● c.1450: this statue of a soldier (below) is made in Padua, Italy, a center of the Italian Renaissance.
● 1453: at the end of the Hundred Years War England keeps only Calais.

● 1291: Crusaders are driven from the Holy Land after the fall of Acre.
● c. 1300: the Ottoman Empire is founded.

● The Ottoman Empire begins its gradual expansion, reaching the fringe of Europe in 1354 with the capture of Gallipoli.
● By the end of the century, the Ottomans control Anatolia and Bulgaria and their empire stretches from the Danube in the west to the Euphrates in the east.

● The Seljuk Turkish Empire expands rapidly. The Seljuks conquer Iran and Iraq and in 1064 attack Constantinople.

● Saladin (right) founds the Ayyubid dynasty and unites the Muslim tribes of Egypt, Syria and Mesopotamia.

● The Ottoman Empire is destroyed by the Mongols, and then rebuilt.
● 1453: Constantinople falls to the Ottomans.

● New states are founded in West Africa, among them the Ife culture (modern Nigeria).
● The first stone buildings appear in Great Zimbabwe.
● Swahili towns on the east African coast grow wealthy from trade between inland Zimbabwean kingdoms and markets across the ocean.

● The first Christian crusades against Muslims in Palestine and Egypt.
● The Ayyubids take power in Egypt.

● This rock-church (below) is cut from the rock in Lalibela, Ethiopia.
● West African gold is used for European coins.

● Zimbabwe culture is at its height.
● Many southern and central African kingdoms are founded.
● Portuguese sailors reach the west coast of Africa.
● The English, French and Dutch trade with West Africa.
● Benin in West Africa is at its height.

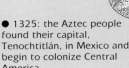

● By 1000 a new dynasty, the Song, controls China. The empire is more peaceful, but threats are growing from abroad.

● 1467: in Japan the beginning of 100 years of civil war, as rival samurai armies fight for control of the country.

● In south-east Asia the Khmer Empire reaches its height under Jayavarman VII. The splendid city of Angkor Wat (above) is built.

● The Mongol Empire under Qubilai Khan reaches its greatest extent. It extends from the Pacific Ocean to the Black Sea.

● The Toltecs have a huge empire in Central America. They worship the Feathered Serpent Quetzalcóatl (above).

● The Mogollon people of southwest North America are building stone houses and round underground ceremonial rooms, called kivas.
● The Anasazi people of Utah, Colorado, New Mexico and Arizona are building pueblos, three- and four-story-high apartment style dwellings.

● The Incas, at this time a small, warlike tribe, settle in an Andean valley in Peru. Gradually they extend their influence and win more territory around their capital city, Cuzco. They make this ceremonial knife (right) out of gold and turquoise. It depicts a richly dressed man.

● 1325: the Aztec people found their capital, Tenochtitlán, in Mexico and begin to colonize Central America.

● The Aztec Empire grows to cover much of Central America.
● The Inca Empire grows rapidly across Peru.

1100   1200   1300   1400   1500

THE SPREAD OF CHRISTIANITY

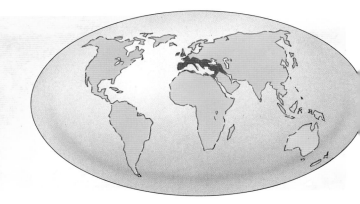

IN 63 BC THE ROMANS conquered Judea, in the eastern Mediterranean. The main inhabitants of Judea were Jews. Many Jews believed that one day a "Messiah," or "Christ," would free them from the Romans.

In about AD 27 a Jewish man called Jesus began preaching in the area north of Judea called Galilee. Jesus said that he was the son of God, and that only people who asked God to forgive their sins would be granted eternal life in heaven. After three years he was brought before a Jewish court and found guilty of offending God. At the order of the Roman governor, Pontius Pilate, Jesus was nailed to a cross and left to die. His followers, or disciples, said that he then appeared to them after rising from the dead. They believed that Jesus was both "Christ" and God, and began to spread the story of his life and teachings.

Stories of Jesus
Jesus Christ's followers, called Christians, spread stories of Jesus by word of mouth, in letters and in accounts of his life. By the 4th century there was a collection of these stories and accounts, called the New Testament. It has been used by Christians ever since as the basis of their faith. This fragment of parchment is the oldest surviving Christian text. It was copied in Egypt in about AD 150.

St. Catherine's monastery in Egypt
This monastery of St. Catherine in Egypt was the house of one of the earliest Christian communities. It was founded in 557, in this remote desert landscape. Christians gave away their belongings and lived together in these communities, where they prayed to God.

Celebrating the Eucharist
Jesus told his followers to meet together and to eat bread and drink wine in memory of his life and death. The Eucharist, or thanksgiving service, has been the main service of most Christian churches ever since.

Key

�	Christianized by AD 325
▢	Christianized by AD 600
—	St. Paul's first route
—	St. Paul's second route
✝	5 Patriarch bases

Sevill

St. Paul
Paul was a Jewish leader who attacked Christians. He then made a dramatic conversion to Christianity in about AD 35. He spread the message of Jesus around the Mediterranean.

The catacombs
The city of Rome, the heart of the empire, had become strongly Christian by early in the 4th century. We can see evidence of this in the places where people buried their dead. By this time land for burials had become more scarce and expensive, so cemeteries, or catacombs, were excavated below ground. They could be several stories extending downward. This is a catacomb, built in the Via Latina, Rome, in the 4th century for an unknown family or group. We do not know who they were, but they must have been wealthy to have had the chambers so lavishly decorated.

In most catacombs the walls and ceilings are covered with religious paintings. Some show scenes and motifs from old pagan religions – such as flowers, birds and cherubs – but most depict Christian motifs and scenes from the Bible – the feeding of the five thousand, or Jesus' baptism. The style of the paintings is similar to that used in pagan art. These early Christian artists used the styles they knew from the past to tell the stories of their new faith. The paintings in this catacomb, which was discovered only in 1955, are some of the best-known examples of early Christian art.

The spread of the Christian faith
Jesus' followers spread the Christian faith from Judea to Antioch in Syria. From here, they carried the story of Jesus to cities around the northeast Mediterranean. As a result, Christians founded new communities throughout the Roman Empire.

The Romans normally allowed people to worship whatever gods they chose. However, the Christians soon ran into problems with the Roman authorities, because Christians refused to worship the emperor of Rome as a god. They said their God was the only true God. Some emperors, such as Nero (AD 54–68), treated them cruelly. Nero ordered Christians to be fed to wild beasts or burned to death. Thousands of Christians were killed. Despite this, Romans continued to convert to Christianity, and the Christian faith grew even stronger.

Then, in 312, an astonishing event changed the position of Christians in the Roman Empire. The emperor Constantine made Christianity the official religion of the Roman Empire. In the next 300 years Christianity grew further. By 600 most villages and towns had their own churches. The churches of an area were governed by a bishop. Above these were leaders called "patriarchs," based at Jerusalem, Alexandria, Antioch, Constantinople and Rome.

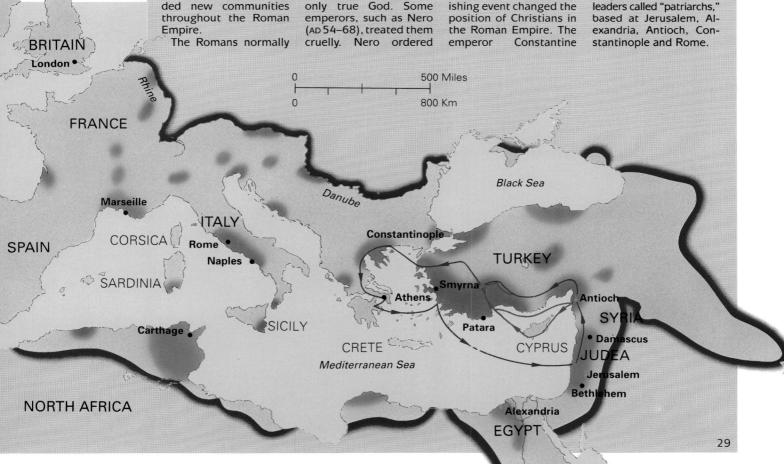

BRITAIN
London
FRANCE
Rhine
Marseille
ITALY
SPAIN
CORSICA
Rome
Naples
SARDINIA
Carthage
SICILY
Danube
Black Sea
Constantinople
TURKEY
Smyrna
Athens
Patara
Antioch
SYRIA
CYPRUS
Damascus
CRETE
JUDEA
Mediterranean Sea
Jerusalem
Bethlehem
Alexandria
NORTH AFRICA
EGYPT

0   500 Miles
0   800 Km

THE BYZANTINE EMPIRE

IN 293 THE ROMAN Empire was divided in two. There was now a Western Empire based in Rome, and an Eastern Empire based in Constantinople (modern Istanbul, in Turkey). Within 200 years invaders had destroyed the Western Empire. The Eastern Empire, however, survived for another thousand years. Its capital, Constantinople, stood on the site of an old Greek town called Byzantium. From this name, historians have called the Eastern Empire the Byzantine Empire and its inhabitants "Byzantines." Byzantines were strongly Christian. They founded many monasteries and churches, and their church services were full of spectacle, incense and hymn singing. The Byzantines persuaded many peoples in eastern Europe and Russia to become Christian. In 1453 Constantinople was captured by Muslim Turks and the Byzantine Empire collapsed. Its form of Christianity survives, however, as the Eastern Orthodox Church.

Russia becomes a Christian country
In 988 the main ruler of Russia, Prince Vladimir of Kiev, sought a new religion for his people. He chose the Byzantine Christian Church, forcing the people to convert. This Christian church of St. Demetrius at Vladimir was built in 1194.

Santa Sophia
The largest and most magnificent Byzantine church was the Church of the Holy Wisdom (Santa Sophia) in Constantinople, built in 532-37. It was later converted into a mosque, an Islamic place of worship.

Cordob

Tangier

Emperor Justinian
Justinian (527-65) was an outstanding Byzantine emperor. He reconquered some lost lands of the Western Roman Empire. He also reformed the government of the Byzantine Empire. He is seen here in a mosaic picture.

Byzantines and the peoples of the Balkans

At first the Byzantine Empire included most of southeast Europe, known as the Balkans. During the 7th century, Slav peoples from northeast Europe moved into the Balkans. They were followed at the end of the century by Bulgars, from around southern Russia. In this painting, Byzantine horsemen are driving Bulgars away from Thessalonica, an important Byzantine city. However, the Bulgars did eventually conquer Byzantine land and create their own empire.

The Byzantine Empire

The Byzantine Empire was made up of lands around the eastern Mediterranean. The Emperor Justinian reconquered many lands lost to invaders in the 5th century, such as northwest Africa, Italy and southeast Spain. Over the next 400 years, the empire fought hard and successfully against Arab armies to keep hold of its territory. After the year 1000, though, Muslim Turks from the east began to seize more and more territory. In 1453 they stood at the gates of Constantinople itself. The Ottoman Turks had an army of 100,000 men that surrounded Constantinople and cut it off from supplies and help. This is called laying siege. The defenders had only 7,000 troops, but they held out for nearly two months. Eventually the Turks broke through the 100-foot walls of the city. Thousands of the inhabitants were killed or sold as slaves. Constantine XI, the last Byzantine emperor, refused to desert the city and died in its burning ruins.

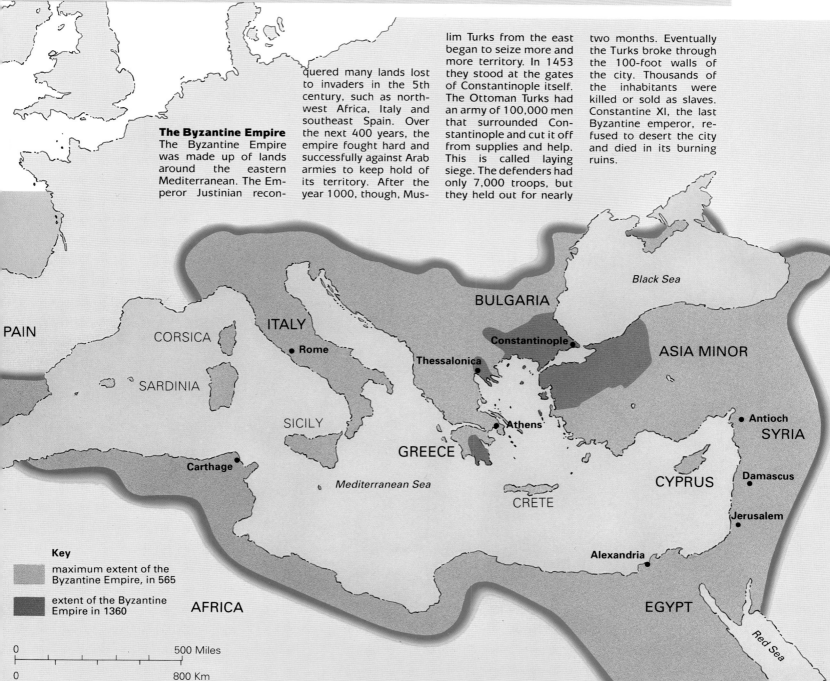

Key

- maximum extent of the Byzantine Empire, in 565
- extent of the Byzantine Empire in 1360

0 — 500 Miles
0 — 800 Km

SPAIN · CORSICA · ITALY · Rome · SARDINIA · SICILY · Carthage · Mediterranean Sea · Thessalonica · GREECE · Athens · CRETE · BULGARIA · Constantinople · Black Sea · ASIA MINOR · CYPRUS · SYRIA · Antioch · Damascus · Jerusalem · Alexandria · AFRICA · EGYPT · Red Sea

THE SPREAD OF ISLAM

I N THE 7TH CENTURY a religion called Islam began in Arabia. It was to sweep across Asia, Africa and into Europe. In 610 Muhammad, from the city of Mecca, claimed he saw visions of an angel, or messenger. This angel brought him messages from God, telling the Arabs that there was only one true God and to stop worshiping false idols, or images of gods. Muhammad urged the people to "accept the will of God," or *Islam* in Arabic, but the Arabs of Mecca rejected his message.

In 622 Muhammad left Mecca. He went to the city of Medina and it became an Islamic community. The two cities then fought each other. In 630 Muhammad was successful: Mecca's idols were destroyed and it became an Islamic city. By the time Muhammad died in 632 his followers, called Muslims, were spreading his teachings.

A Muslim holy man or "sufi"

The man reading from the Muslim holy book, the Quran, is a holy man, or "sufi." The word sufi comes from the Arabic for the simple woolen garment a Muslim holy man wore. The teachings of these sufis were important in spreading Islam through parts of Africa and southern and southeast Asia.

The spread of the Islamic Empire

Muhammad died in 632. His followers chose one of his companions as leader of the Muslims. He was called "caliph," which means successor. At this time Islam was the only faith in Arabia. Outside Arabia the main powers were the Byzantine Empire and a new Persian Empire. Under the early caliphs, Arabian Muslim armies created an empire by conquering the lands controlled by these two empires.

From 661 to 750, the caliphs were all members of the Umayyad family. They ruled from Damascus in Syria, and their armies conquered Spain in the west and expanded as far east as modern Pakistan. The Umayyads were good organizers. They introduced the Arabic language into the captured lands, they started the first Arab coinage, and they developed a postal system, using riders on horseback. All this enabled them to keep their empire together.

However, non-Arab Muslims in these conquered lands resented the way they were treated. In 750 the Persians rebelled against the Umayyads. They helped to establish the rule of the Abbasids, from the city of Baghdad, who ruled until 1258. In that year Baghdad was sacked and the caliph killed by Mongols from central Asia.

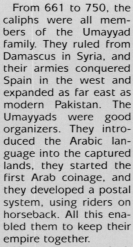

Atlantic Ocean

FRANCE

Arles

SPAIN
Toledo

Tangier

Carthag

The Great Mosque at Damascus

The Great Mosque at Damascus was built in 705-11. It is the oldest surviving large mosque. The prophet Muhammad called on people to honor God in prayer, and so mosques were built wherever Islam spread. In every mosque there is a wall with a hole cut into it. This hole shows the direction of Mecca, the holy city where Islam was born. Muslims always pray in the direction of Mecca.

The Quran

Muhammad wrote down the words of angels who brought him messages from Allah (God), and he also told them to others. After the death of Muhammad, these accounts were gathered together into a book called the Quran. The first official version of the Quran was written by order of the third Muslim caliph, Othman, who was elected caliph in 644. It was the first book to be written in Arabic, and it contains 114 chapters. All but one begin: In the name of Allah, the Most Merciful, the Most Kind. The text of the Quran has always been copied with great care because it is such a holy book.

The Quran speaks of the power of God, or Allah. It tells people to accept his will and to praise him. It instructs Muslims to be kind, to pray, and not to eat during the day for one month in every year. (Children, the sick and the elderly are not included in the command to fast.) They are also instructed to make a religious journey, or pilgrimage, to the holy city of Mecca. These religious duties make up what Muslims call the "Five Pillars." These are: declaring your belief in God; praying; fasting; giving to charity; and pilgrimage to Mecca. "Jihad" or Holy War is sometimes added as another pillar of the faith. This is the duty to spread Islam or defend it against attack.

Islamic books and studies

In this painting a pharmacist is preparing medicines. Around it is an Arabic translation of an ancient Greek book on medicinal plants. The translation was made in Baghdad in the 13th century. Muslim rulers and scholars were interested in subjects such as philosophy and science. Several of the towns and cities brought into the Islamic Empire were already centers of study. So Muslim scholars translated many writings from Greek, Persian and Indian into Arabic. These were then read by Muslim scholars and students throughout the Islamic Empire. Islamic scholars not only studied the ideas of other thinkers but also developed their own ideas on a range of subjects: philosophy, mathematics, astronomy, geography and medicine.

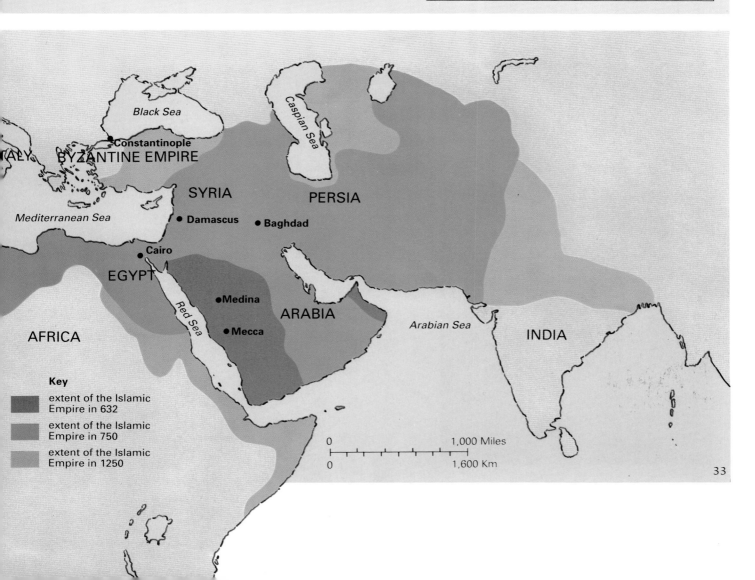

Key
- extent of the Islamic Empire in 632
- extent of the Islamic Empire in 750
- extent of the Islamic Empire in 1250

BARBARIAN EUROPE

THE ROMANS CALLED people who lived outside the empire "barbarians." The word comes from the Latin for "foreigner." Among these barbarians were German tribes such as the Franks, Saxons, Vandals and Goths, and Asian tribes farther to the east, such as the Huns. Toward the end of the 4th century, the Huns invaded Europe. The Goths and Vandals had to flee into the Roman Empire to escape. The Romans agreed to let them settle in the empire as long as they helped defend it against the Huns. But eventually these Germanic tribes realized that the empire was too weak to defend itself any longer. In 410 Alaric the Goth seized Rome, and other tribes grabbed other parts of the empire, establishing their own kingdoms. The most important was that of Clovis, king of the Franks. Between 486 and 507 he conquered Gaul (France). His descendants ruled there until 751, when they were overthrown by a new dynasty, the Carolingians.

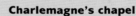

King Recceswinth's crown
This crown of gold and sapphires was given to a church in central Spain by King Recceswinth. He ruled one of the Gothic kingdoms of Spain from 649 to 672. Barbarians loved precious metals and jewels. Their skilled craftsmen could cast silver and gold to make brooches and weapons with intricate designs. They decorated these items with small pieces of colored glass or precious stones.

Charlemagne's chapel
Charlemagne was a Carolingian king of the Franks. He tried to be as grand as the Roman and Byzantine emperors. At Aachen he built a palace based on the Byzantine emperor's palace in Constantinople. Its chapel was a copy of a Byzantine church in Ravenna, Italy.

A barbarian king's hall
The barbarian kings who moved into the Western Roman Empire did not live in cities as the Romans did. They preferred to live on estates in the countryside, and would move from one estate to another. Each estate had a large wooden hall where kings gave feasts.

Charlemagne: Charles the Great

Charlemagne (768-814) was barbarian Europe's most effective ruler. He expanded his kingdom of Francia and created a new empire. Throughout his reign he was involved in war, usually against neighboring peoples. In 800, on Christmas Day, Pope Leo III crowned him Emperor of the West. The school he began in his capital of Aachen became the most important center of learning in western Europe. All this helped to earn him the title "Charlemagne," Charles the Great.

Charlemagne's empire

Toward the end of the 8th century, Charlemagne added parts of modern Germany, Austria, Italy and Spain to his empire. On the borders he created "marches," areas where officers were put in charge of defense. Because his empire was too big for him to run on his own, Charlemagne gave parts of it to nobles and bishops, who ruled in his name. While he was alive, Charlemagne could make sure these men obeyed him. But after his death, in 814, his successors were unable to keep the empire from gradually breaking up. Princes, noblemen and bishops seized the land for themselves and defied the power of the new emperor.

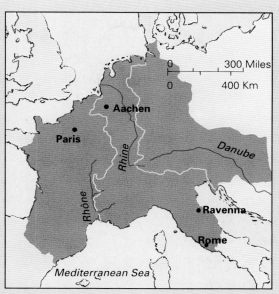

In 843 the empire was divided into three kingdoms, each with its own ruler. (The eastern kingdom later became a separate German Empire).

The empire's problems took a turn for the worse when attacks from another invading people, the Vikings, began.

Barbarian movements

When the Huns began moving into Europe in about 370, other barbarrian tribes poured over the frontier of the weakening Roman Empire. One group of Goths, the Visigoths, sacked Rome in 410 and moved on to settle in southern Spain. Another, the Ostrogoths, held much of Italy. The Vandals came across Europe, moved down through Spain and took control of northwest Africa. By about 475 the Franks, Visigoths and Burgundians ruled most of Gaul (France), and the Angles, Saxons and Jutes had occupied parts of Britain.

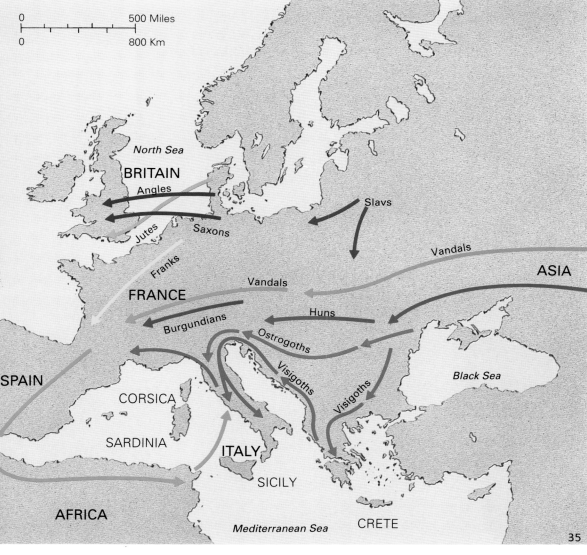

THE VIKING EXPANSION

A T THE END OF the 8th century, the people of Britain, France and Ireland faced a terrible new threat. Raiders arrived by sea from Norway, and began to attack villages, towns, churches and monasteries, stealing anything of value. During the next 200 years Norwegians, Danes and Swedes raided many parts of Europe. They were known as Vikings, or Northmen, and people throughout Europe came to fear them.

Vikings often settled in the countries they raided. The growing population of Norway and the lack of farmland there drove many young men to seek adventure and wealth abroad. In the 9th century, Danes raided and settled in Ireland, Britain and France. People from Sweden set up a large kingdom in eastern Europe, and gave the area their own name of "Rus." This is how the name "Russia" originated. The Vikings also started settlements in Greenland, and from there it is thought they may have sailed to North America.

Norwegians in Iceland Norwegians discovered the island they named "Ice land" in about 860 and by 930 about 20,000 of them had settled there. Their government was an assembly of leading men. It was called the "althing," and it met once a year on this plain (above).

Oseberg animal head This fierce animal head may have been part of a Viking chair. It was found in a Viking ship-grave at Oseberg in Norway. Also at the site were four sleds, beds, a tapestry and other items including the ship itself (opposite page). Scandinavians were frequently buried with their possessions, to use in the afterlife, and with offerings for the gods.

A Viking village in America Two Icelandic histories tell of how some Vikings sailing to Greenland lost their way, and saw a country to the west of Greenland. Later, other Vikings visited this country and tried to settle there. Had they found America? No one knew until 1960, when an archaeologist discovered remains of this small village in Newfoundland, Canada. It was begun in about AD 1000, but was not lived in for long. It had five houses, a smithy (blacksmith's workshop), a kiln (furnace) for making charcoal, and boat sheds. The Vikings named the land where they briefly settled "Vinland" (Wine Land) because of the grapes that were supposed to grow there.

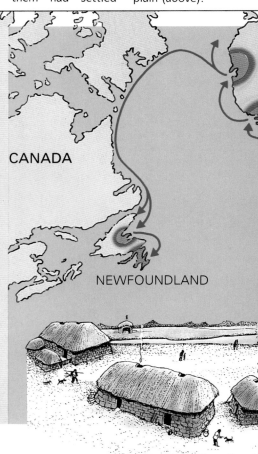

CANADA

NEWFOUNDLAND

Viking ships

The Vikings were able to sail across wide oceans and then up narrow and shallow rivers because they built superb ships. This ship was found in a burial mound at Oseberg, in Norway. It dates from about 800 and is the oldest surviving Viking ship. Viking ships were long and narrow, and had a shallow draft. This means they did not need deep water to sail in. Just as importantly, they could be dragged easily onto the shore and across land from one river to another. This enabled Vikings to travel deep into a country by sailing up its rivers. They built their ships with oak planks, and sometimes decorated the sides and fronts with carvings.

A typical Viking ship has at least 20 pairs of oars and a sail. This means that most of their ships had a crew of 40 men or more. Some Viking raiding parties had 200 ships in them and the one which attacked Paris in 886 had a fleet of 700 ships! The Vikings gave their ships and their swords names. Common names for swords were "skull splitter" and "brain biter."

Viking expeditions

The Vikings were brave and skillful sailors. Norwegians regularly sailed to Greenland and back, for almost 2,000 miles each way. Swedes sailed from the kingdom of Rus and discovered routes to the Byzantine and Islamic Empires. They traded in furs, semiprecious stones such as amber, honey and slaves. Danish Vikings settled in England at the end of the 9th century and conquered most of the country. Only the English kingdom of Wessex, under King Alfred, held out. However, by the early 11th century the Danes had gained control of all of England. At about the same time the people of Scandinavia, Iceland and Greenland stopped their raids. They now helped to make the area they controlled richer through an increase in trade, across the Atlantic Ocean and the Baltic Sea to the lands beyond.

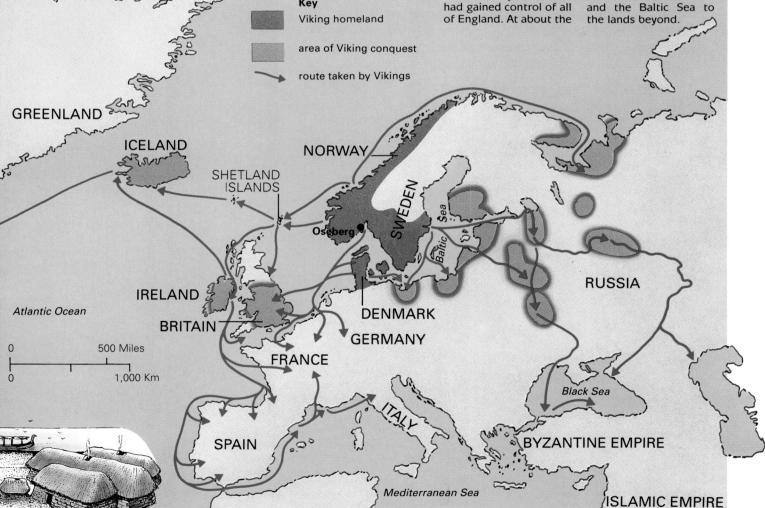

Key

Viking homeland

area of Viking conquest

route taken by Vikings

GREENLAND

ICELAND

SHETLAND ISLANDS

NORWAY

SWEDEN

Baltic Sea

Oseberg

IRELAND

BRITAIN

Atlantic Ocean

0   500 Miles

0   1,000 Km

DENMARK

GERMANY

FRANCE

RUSSIA

SPAIN

ITALY

Black Sea

BYZANTINE EMPIRE

Mediterranean Sea

ISLAMIC EMPIRE

MEDIEVAL EUROPE

THE PERIOD OF history known as the Middle Ages (or medieval period) lasted from about 500 to about 1500. During the 9th and 10th centuries western Europe was attacked by Vikings, Magyars (modern-day Hungarians) and Muslim pirates, called Saracens. By 1000 these attacks had stopped.

The high Middle Ages (12th–13th centuries) were prosperous years in Europe. The main reason for this was the improvement in agriculture. Warmer weather and inventions such as the windmill and water-mill helped to increase the amount of food produced. More land was used for farming, and forests were chopped down to make new fields. Rulers and the Catholic Church spent their increased wealth on building more castles, cathedrals and monasteries. Even villagers and townspeople were rich enough to build their own churches.

The growth of towns
The town of Rothenburg in Germany, shown in this picture, was built in the medieval period, and its size and layout are typical of a medieval town. Between 1000 and 1300 Europe's population more than doubled, to over 80 million. So the rulers of Europe built over 4,000 new towns. New buildings were put up outside the walls as the towns grew. Towns became centers of trade. By 1300 western Europe's largest cities were Paris, Milan, Florence, Venice and Naples, each with about 100,000 people. In these cities trade and culture flourished, but they were also crowded and dirty, and disease was rife.

Laon, a Gothic cathedral
Laon cathedral, in France, was built between 1160 and 1225. It was built in the style of architecture called Gothic, which included features such as tall, thin columns and pointed arches, stretching up as if to heaven. Its windows were made of beautifully colored pieces of glass.

Europe in 1500
For most of the Middle Ages, Europe was a mixture of kingdoms and lands ruled by nobles. Most Europeans were Catholic Christians, and the Church, led by the Pope, helped to bring the peoples of Europe together. The language of the Church was Latin, and religious people used it as a common language throughout Europe.

By 1500 there were three strong kingdoms in Europe: England, France and Castile in Spain. The peoples of these countries all shared the same religion and each had a sense of national identity.

On the other hand, German land (called the Holy Roman Empire) was divided into many different states. German emperors had allowed nobles, bishops and towns to govern themselves and so there was no real central control.

PORTUGAL

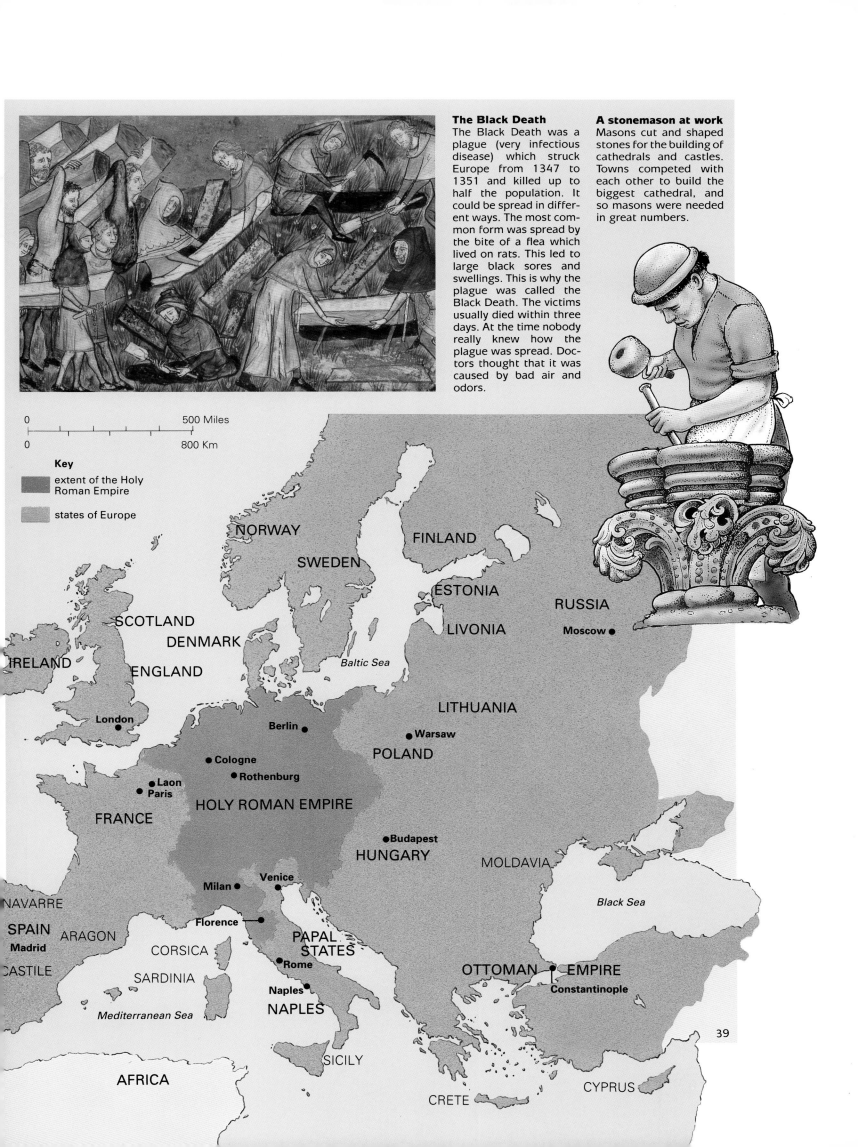

The Black Death

The Black Death was a plague (very infectious disease) which struck Europe from 1347 to 1351 and killed up to half the population. It could be spread in different ways. The most common form was spread by the bite of a flea which lived on rats. This led to large black sores and swellings. This is why the plague was called the Black Death. The victims usually died within three days. At the time nobody really knew how the plague was spread. Doctors thought that it was caused by bad air and odors.

A stonemason at work

Masons cut and shaped stones for the building of cathedrals and castles. Towns competed with each other to build the biggest cathedral, and so masons were needed in great numbers.

0   500 Miles

0   800 Km

Key

extent of the Holy Roman Empire

states of Europe

NORWAY

SWEDEN

FINLAND

ESTONIA

RUSSIA

LIVONIA

Moscow ●

SCOTLAND

DENMARK

IRELAND

ENGLAND

Baltic Sea

LITHUANIA

London ●

Berlin ●

Warsaw ●

POLAND

● Cologne

● Rothenburg

● Laon

● Paris

HOLY ROMAN EMPIRE

FRANCE

● Budapest

HUNGARY

MOLDAVIA

Milan ●   Venice ●

Black Sea

NAVARRE

Florence ●

SPAIN   ARAGON

CORSICA

PAPAL STATES

Madrid

● Rome

CASTILE

SARDINIA

OTTOMAN ● EMPIRE

Constantinople

Naples ●

Mediterranean Sea

NAPLES

39

AFRICA

SICILY

CYPRUS

CRETE

THE SPREAD OF BUDDHISM

BUDDHISM WAS begun in India by Gautama Siddhartha in the 6th century BC. He was a wealthy Indian prince who turned his back on riches to search for a more meaningful way of life. He wanted to know why there was so much suffering in the world. He found the answer through deep thought, called meditation. He said that through meditation it was possible to reach a state of perfect peace, called "nirvana." He was therefore called the Buddha, which means "the Enlightened One."

The Buddha taught that everything in the world is connected. True happiness can be achieved only when we respect the life of every living thing, and when we are generous and kind. If we harm others, then we harm ourselves too. Buddhism spread quickly across northern India because it was a religion for all people, rich and poor alike. In the 3rd century BC, Ashoka, the emperor of India, became a Buddhist, and the religion spread to southern India and Sri Lanka (previously called Ceylon).

Guanyin, a Chinese goddess
There are two main branches of the Buddhist religion: Theravada and Mahayana. Theravada Buddhism has simple rituals and customs, while Mahayana has more elaborate ones. The Chinese goddess Guanyin is seen here in a 10th-century cave painting. She is worshiped by Mahayana Buddhists. Theravada Buddhists believe only *the* Buddha can show the way to enlightenment.

Statue of Buddha
This statue of the dying Buddha, at peace with the world, comes from Sri Lanka. Sri Lanka is the country where Buddhism has survived the longest. It arrived over 2,200 years ago, at the end of the 3rd century BC. Buddhist monks in Sri Lanka during the 1st century BC wrote down Buddha's teachings, and the medieval kings of Sri Lanka later built Buddhist shrines and monasteries in his honor. Many still exist today.

Buddhist monks
Buddhist monks explain the teachings of Buddha, and people bring them food and clothing. They own very little and depend on these gifts.

The Buddhist temple at Borobudur

One of the most magnificent and elaborate of all Buddhist buildings is the great temple at Borobudur in Java. It was probably built in about AD 800 for the king of Java. It has the shape of a pyramid, with five square platforms. Each platform is surrounded by a wall. On the insides of the walls are panels with detailed carvings, showing scenes from the lives of Buddha and of a Buddhist pilgrim. In total there are about 1,300 carved panels. At the top of the temple is a "stupa,"

a mound built to contain holy relics. It is surrounded by 72 small bell-shaped shrines, each containing a statue of Buddha. The stupa is the most sacred type of Buddhist building. In Japan, the stupa developed into the pagoda (see opposite page, top left).

The Borobudur temple is meant to represent the Buddhist life. Its square shape represents the universe. As the visitor climbs up through the different levels of the temple, it is like climbing toward the state of Buddhist enlightenment or "nirvana."

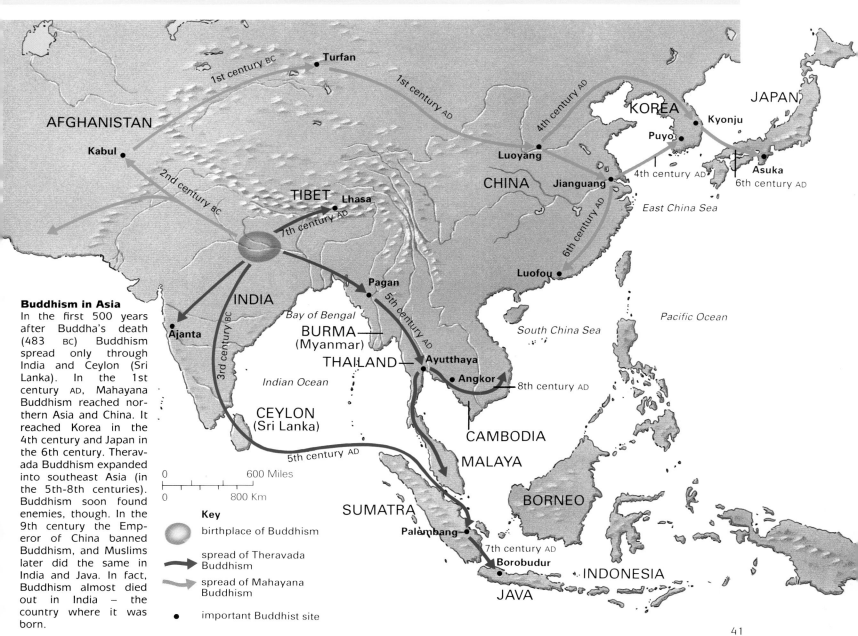

Buddhism in Asia

In the first 500 years after Buddha's death (483 BC) Buddhism spread only through India and Ceylon (Sri Lanka). In the 1st century AD, Mahayana Buddhism reached northern Asia and China. It reached Korea in the 4th century and Japan in the 6th century. Theravada Buddhism expanded into southeast Asia (in the 5th-8th centuries). Buddhism soon found enemies, though. In the 9th century the Emperor of China banned Buddhism, and Muslims later did the same in India and Java. In fact, Buddhism almost died out in India – the country where it was born.

Key
- 🔘 birthplace of Buddhism
- ➡ spread of Theravada Buddhism
- ➡ spread of Mahayana Buddhism
- • important Buddhist site

0 ———— 600 Miles
0 ———— 800 Km

MEDIEVAL CHINA

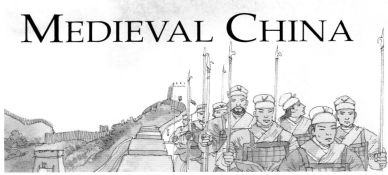

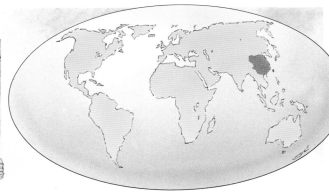

FOR HUNDREDS of years China was ruled by different dynasties. A dynasty is a succession of rulers who all come from the same family. China was first united under one ruler between 221 BC and AD 311 (see page 18). In the next 1,000 years China was divided and reunited three times. The third time was in 960, when the first Song emperor reunited the country. During the Song dynasty there were great developments in China. Technology advanced more quickly than in Europe. The Chinese had firearms and bombs, made clocks, and used compasses and paper money long before Europeans. They also invented the first machine for recording earthquakes. They even had a form of vaccination against disease, which was not developed in Europe until the 18th century.

In 1279 the Song dynasty was finally overthrown by Mongol tribesmen from the north, and China came under foreign rule for the first time. From then on, China's interest in new ideas and learning declined.

Street life in Kaifeng
This picture shows the busy world of Kaifeng in north China in about 1100. At that time Kaifeng was the capital of China, with a popula-tion of perhaps 1 million. The city was a busy trading center. People carried their goods to market on special wheel-barrows and in sacks attached to poles.

Papermaking
From about AD 105 an important Chinese invention was paper-making. Their method was to soak tree bark and bamboo shoots in water. This mixture was then beaten into a pulp. Finally the pulp was lifted out of the water on a screen (below, left) and laid out to dry, forming a sheet (below, right).

Chinese temple
Buddhism reached China in the 1st century AD, and flourished there be-tween the 5th and 9th centuries. The temple pictured above was built in the 6th century. It was designed in the pagoda style, which originated in India. The heavy tiled roofs are supported by columns resting on raised plat-forms.

In the mid-9th cen-tury the Tang emperor turned against Bud-dhism. He seized Bud-dhist buildings. The religion still managed to survive in China, but only as the faith of a minority of people.

Canals in China

Canals like this one in Suzhou were important for Chinese trade and communication. The emperors used them to transport rice from the south to feed their armies based in the north, because it was often too difficult and dangerous to bring it by sea. Many of these canals are still in use today. In the 10th century the Chinese invented the pound lock. Locks allowed the water level to be raised or lowered so that barges could continue their journey.

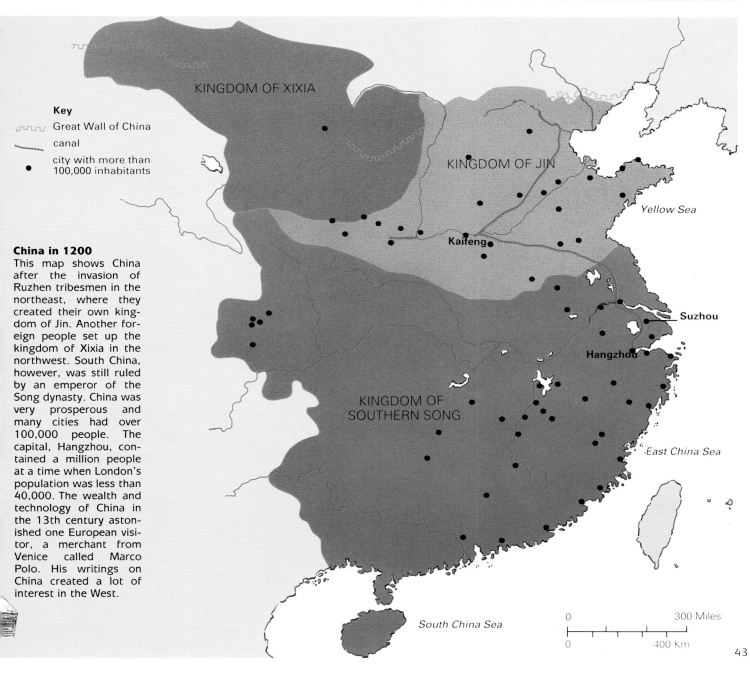

Key

〜〜〜 Great Wall of China

—— canal

● city with more than 100,000 inhabitants

KINGDOM OF XIXIA

KINGDOM OF JIN

Yellow Sea

Kaifeng

Suzhou

Hangzhou

KINGDOM OF SOUTHERN SONG

East China Sea

South China Sea

0 ——————— 300 Miles

0 ——————— 400 Km

China in 1200

This map shows China after the invasion of Ruzhen tribesmen in the northeast, where they created their own kingdom of Jin. Another foreign people set up the kingdom of Xixia in the northwest. South China, however, was still ruled by an emperor of the Song dynasty. China was very prosperous and many cities had over 100,000 people. The capital, Hangzhou, contained a million people at a time when London's population was less than 40,000. The wealth and technology of China in the 13th century astonished one European visitor, a merchant from Venice called Marco Polo. His writings on China created a lot of interest in the West.

THE MONGOL EXPANSION

THE MONGOLS were tribesmen from northeast Asia. They were fierce and excellent horsemen, and won stunning victories against much bigger enemy forces. The Mongol Empire grew very quickly under the leadership of Temuchin, and in about 1200 he was given the title of Chinghiz Khan (Genghis Khan), or "Universal Ruler." He had swept into central Asia and northern China by 1215. His greatest achievement was to unite the different Mongol tribes, and to give them all – even the Khan himself – one set of laws. He built a terrifying and efficient army. His bowmen could kill at a distance of 590 feet and his horsemen once covered 275 miles in three days. After his death in 1227, his empire was divided among his four sons and grandson. The areas they ruled were called khanates. By 1258 they had added Russia, southern China and Baghdad to the Mongol Empire, making it the largest empire ever created.

Mongols attack Baghdad

A famous Mongol victory was the capture of Baghdad in 1258, shown here. Baghdad was the capital of the Islamic Empire and home of its head, or caliph. It was a walled city. When they invaded a city, the Mongols usually offered to spare the lives of its inhabitants if they would surrender immediately. If they refused, the Mongols threatened to massacre them. When the Mongols attacked a city they used siege engineers. These were men who dug under the walls of the city to make them collapse. The people of Baghdad refused to surrender at first, and fought the Mongols. Eventually they surrendered, and thousands were killed.

The Mongol Empire

The Mongol Empire was at its largest in the middle of the 13th century. The death of the Great Khan, Mongke, in 1259, led to quarreling between the other khanates and the breakup of the empire. In the west there were the Ilkhanate of Persia and the Chagatai Khanate. In 1260 Qubilai Khan (Kublai Khan), a grandson of Chinghiz, took over the Great Khanate, which comprised much of China. Then in 1279 he secured control of the wealthy Song Empire in south China. He established himself as the first of the Yuan imperial dynasty, and moved its center from the north to Beijing – where the capital of China still is today.

Although the Mongols are remembered as a fierce and merciless people, their empire also brought a long period of peace and stability to a vast area. This led to a flourishing trade between many lands, and Marco Polo was one of many Italian merchants who benefited from it. The Mongols were clever enough to realize that trade made the people of their empire wealthy. That wealth was taxed by the khans, and so everyone did well. However, just one century later the empire broke up as new rulers seized their lands. China was lost in 1367 and there were defeats in the west in 1380. The Khanate of the Golden Horde was the last to fall in 1502.

Key

— extent of the Mongol Empire in 1259

– – – addition to the Mongol Empire in 1279

Life in Mongolia

The Mongols were a nomadic people who moved regularly through their land. Much of this land was open grassland, or "steppe." Here they kept flocks of sheep which provided them with meat, milk and skins. They used the sheepskins to make their tents, called yurts, by stretching them over wooden frames. Nomadic herders of today still drive their sheep to new pastures, and yurts are still their shelter. The tents are cone-shaped, easy to assemble, transport and reerect. They are cool in summer, but keep out the cold of winter. Every autumn herders would move their flocks of sheep to the mountain valleys, in order to find shelter for the winter.

Chinghiz Khan chases his enemies

Chinghiz Khan was able to conquer huge territories because he created a ferocious and disciplined army, more powerful than any in Europe. They fought with swords (as in this picture), lances and very powerful bows. The Mongol cavalry was the key to this success. They were fast and skillful horsemen, who were able to cover up to 100 miles a day. The army may have contained 100,000 men, supplied with half a million horses. Most of these men were Turks, so the Turkish people and language followed Chinghiz Khan's army westward as the empire expanded. The settlement of the Turks throughout the region helped to prepare the way for the formation, later, of the Ottoman Empire (see page 58).

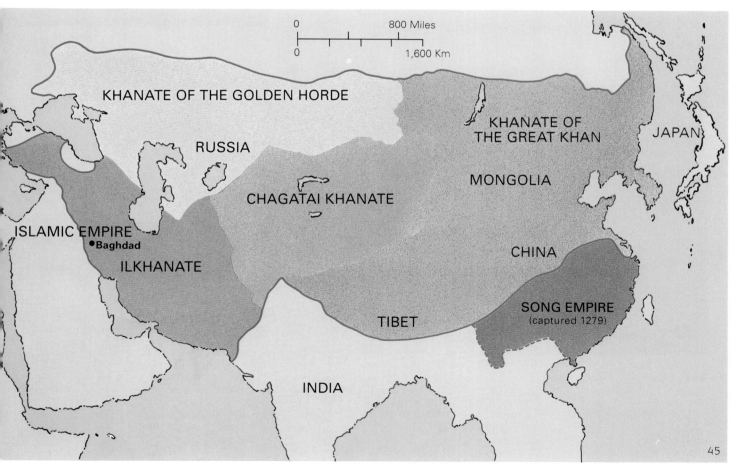

AFRICAN KINGDOMS

HUMAN BEINGS first evolved in Africa, and it was here that stone tools were developed and the hunter-gatherer way of life began. The introduction of agriculture from the Middle East meant that people gradually stopped living in small hunter-gatherer groups and began to live in settlements surrounded by fields. The introduction of iron-working, also from the Middle East, allowed people to make more efficient tools and weapons. The settlements grew and trade between them began.

In the 7th century AD the Arabs invaded North Africa (see page 32), converting the people to Islam, and set up trading routes across the Sahara desert. This helped in the creation of large trading kingdoms in West Africa. These kingdoms, which had their own systems of government and their own armies, traded between themselves and sold gold and spices to the Arab traders. They also produced much fine art. Some of the people from West Africa migrated southward and established settlements throughout the rest of Africa.

Great Zimbabwe
Some of the African peoples who settled in eastern and southern Africa established kingdoms. The most important of these was the kingdom of Monomotapa, which flourished from the 10th to the 15th centuries. Its capital was Great Zimbabwe, whose stone walls, enclosures and towers still survive as ruins today. The rulers of Great Zimbabwe became rich because they controlled the mining and export of gold in the region.

The churches of Abyssinia
Abyssinia (now Ethiopia) was the oldest kingdom in Africa. No one knows when it began but, high up in the mountains and surrounded by desert, it was not conquered until the 20th century. It became a Christian country in the 4th century and it is still Christian today. Among its treasures are the eleven "rock churches" at Lalibela. They were cut out of solid rock. This one, the church of St. George, was probably built in the 13th century.

A bronze water pot
This bronze roped pot was found at a burial site at Igbo Ukwu, in Benin. It was probably made in the 9th century, and used for holding water. It stands about one foot tall. The rope around the pot is made of delicately twisted bronze threads.

Camels in the Sahara

The giant Sahara Desert separates North Africa from West Africa. It is 3,000 miles wide and 1,200 miles deep. Arab traders carried their goods across the Sahara on camels in groups like this one, called caravans. Camels can go for many days without water and this was very important as it took two months to travel across the desert.

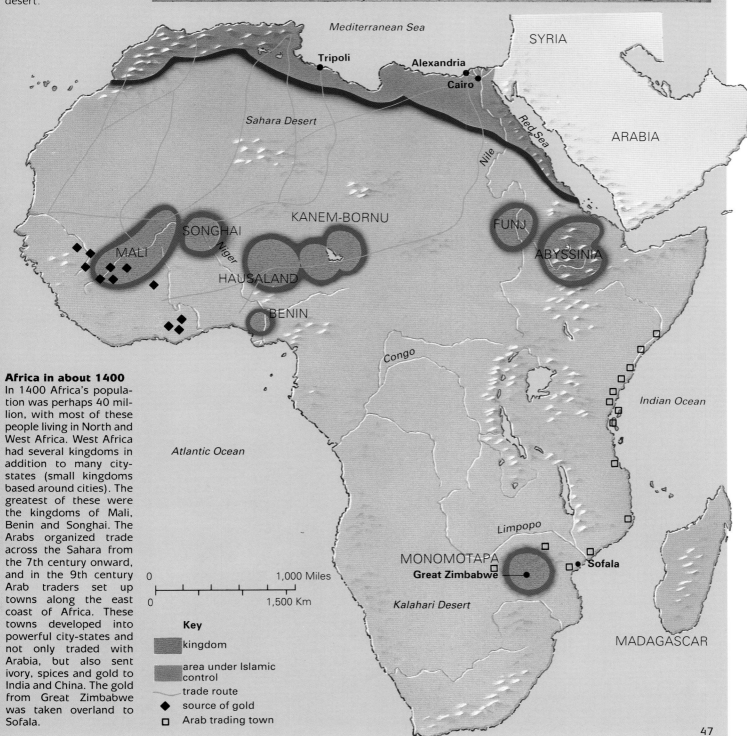

Mediterranean Sea

SYRIA

Tripoli

Alexandria

Cairo

Sahara Desert

Red Sea

ARABIA

Nile

KANEM-BORNU

SONGHAI

FUNJ

MALI

ABYSSINIA

Niger

HAUSALAND

BENIN

Congo

Indian Ocean

Atlantic Ocean

Limpopo

MONOMOTAPA

Sofala

Great Zimbabwe

Kalahari Desert

MADAGASCAR

Africa in about 1400

In 1400 Africa's population was perhaps 40 million, with most of these people living in North and West Africa. West Africa had several kingdoms in addition to many city-states (small kingdoms based around cities). The greatest of these were the kingdoms of Mali, Benin and Songhai. The Arabs organized trade across the Sahara from the 7th century onward, and in the 9th century Arab traders set up towns along the east coast of Africa. These towns developed into powerful city-states and not only traded with Arabia, but also sent ivory, spices and gold to India and China. The gold from Great Zimbabwe was taken overland to Sofala.

| 0 | 1,000 Miles |
| 0 | 1,500 Km |

Key

▦ kingdom

▦ area under Islamic control

— trade route

◆ source of gold

□ Arab trading town

47

NATIVE EMPIRES OF AMERICA

THE EARLY AMERICANS were hunters, fishers and food gatherers. Farming first began in an area called "Mesoamerica," which includes Central America and Mexico. Two of the earliest civilizations grew up in Mesoamerica and South America in about 1200 BC – the Olmec civilization in Mexico and the first civilization of the central Andes in what is now Peru. Civilization in Mesoamerica reached its peak with the Maya in Central America. The Maya were expert mathematicians and astronomers. Their civilization lasted from 300 BC to the 16th century. Another civilization which flourished in the area at the same time was that of Teotihuacán. Teotihuacán was Mesoamerica's first real city. In AD 600 it covered about 8 square miles and had a population of about 150,000, living in homes similar to apartment houses. Later, in the mid-14th century, the Aztecs created an empire which stretched across central Mexico. In the central Andes, the Inca civilization began in about 1200 and reached its peak in the middle of the 15th century.

South American cloth
Native South Americans produced some of the most intricate and colorful cloths ever made. Some surviving pieces of cloth have almost 200 different colors. The people had learned to make cloth with cotton by 3000 BC. Later they also used wool from llamas and other animals. The cloth would have been woven on this portable "backstrap loom" (below). The most elaborate cloths would have been used to decorate temples, palaces and other important buildings.

Maya civilization
The Maya Indians produced the most splendid native American civilization, in the region north of modern Guatemala. The Maya civilization was at its peak between AD 300 and 800. The Maya built their cities in the rainforests of the lowlands. Here the remarkable plazas, steeply stepped pyramids, and palaces were used for religious ceremonies. This temple-pyramid was discovered at the site of a city called Chichén Itzá. It is decorated with sculptures and inscriptions.

For reasons we do not yet know, the cities were abandoned in about 900, but the Maya civilization continued further to the north, in modern Mexico.

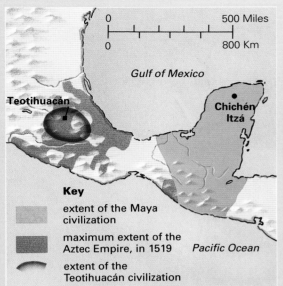

Key

extent of the Maya civilization

maximum extent of the Aztec Empire, in 1519

extent of the Teotihuacán civilization

Mesoamerica

The civilizations of Mesoamerica (above), in Central America, had many common features, such as the building of ceremonial centers, the worship of similar gods, and the playing of a ball game (top, left).

An Inca city

Machu Picchu is the best-preserved Inca city. It sits in a spectacular position on a ridge 9,840 feet high in the Andes Mountains. Its buildings include a royal palace and three temples. Around the ridge are narrow terraces on which the Incas grew food. The city remained undiscovered until 1911.

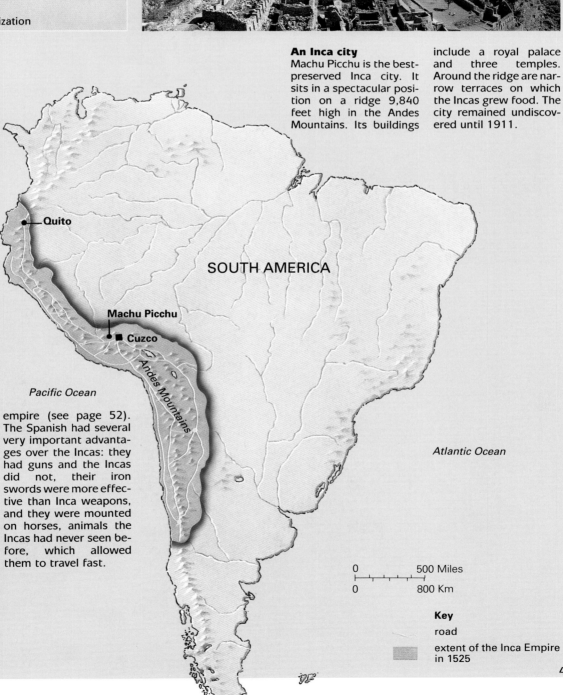

The Inca Empire

From about 1440 the Incas began to increase their empire by conquest, until by 1515 it stretched for nearly 2,500 miles and contained as many as 12 million people. The empire had two capitals, one at Cuzco and another, Quito, in the north. It was linked together by perhaps as many as 6,200 miles of roads. Because they had no horses, the Incas used messengers to communicate across the long, narrow empire. They operated on a relay system, and had to cross deep gorges using the many amazing suspension bridges.

The Spanish began their invasion of the Incas in 1532, and took only three years to conquer the whole empire (see page 52). (see page 52) The Spanish had several very important advantages over the Incas: they had guns and the Incas did not, their iron swords were more effective than Inca weapons, and they were mounted on horses, animals the Incas had never seen before, which allowed them to travel fast.

Key

road

extent of the Inca Empire in 1525

EMPIRES AROUND THE WORLD

North and South America, Africa and the Far East open up to the Europeans. Europe itself is divided by religious conflict.

EUROPE

● The Reformation, begun by Martin Luther in 1517, takes hold in much of Germany, Sweden, Denmark and Norway. England adopts its own version of Protestantism.
● Charles V (right), Holy Roman emperor (1519–56), is involved in a bitter struggle with France to dominate Europe.

● 1543: Nicolaus Copernicus, a Pole, first claims that the Earth moves around the Sun and not the other way around.

● The Catholic Church begins its own campaign against the ideas of the Reformation, called the Counter-Reformation.

● In France the Wars of Religion rage between the Catholics and the French Protestants, called Huguenots.

● 1618–48: the Thirty Years War, which begins as a religious quarrel between Catholics and Protestants in the Holy Roman Empire, becomes a power struggle to control Europe.
● In England the Civil War between Parliament and King Charles I ends in a victory for Parliament. Charles I is executed in

MIDDLE EAST

● The war between the Ottoman Empire and Venice is over by 1502. It has established the Ottomans (below) as a sea power.

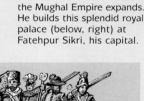

● Suleiman the Magnificent (1520–66) (above) ruled the vast Ottoman Empire in its golden age.
● Another Middle Eastern

Muslim state, the Safavid Empire of Persia, emerges. There is religious conflict between them and the Ottomans.

● Janissaries (below) are the Ottoman sultans' bodyguard.
● 1629: after the death of Abbas I, the Safavid dynasty declines.

AFRICA

● The 50 years to 1550 see the rapid growth of the slave trade, as Europeans plunder the coast of Africa for slaves

to work for them in the West Indies.
● 1518: the first of these human cargoes is transported from West Africa.

● 1562: the first English cargo of slaves is transported from West Africa by Hawkins.
● The Portuguese colonize part of Angola, but their control over northwestern Africa is ended by the Moroccans.
● 1591: the Moroccans destroy the West African empire of Songhai.

● The influence of Portugal on Africa shows in this sculpture of a Portuguese soldier made by a West African craftsman (below).

● 1625: a new kingdom, Dahomey, is created along the West African coast by King Akaba, but elsewhere the European influence

ASIA AND AUSTRALASIA

● After Vasco da Gama's voyage to India in 1498, Europeans open up trade routes with the Far East. They come into contact

with native civilizations, such as the natives of Papua New Guinea (below, left). Christian missionaries soon follow the traders.

● Under Akbar the Great the Mughal Empire expands. He builds this splendid royal palace (below, right) at Fatehpur Sikri, his capital.

● 1615: the Dutch seize the Moluccas from the Portuguese. They are the only Europeans allowed to trade with Japan.

NORTH AND SOUTH AMERICA

● 1519: Hernán Cortes and his 500 men arrive among the Aztecs in Mexico. By 1521 the whole empire has been taken.

● The Spanish conquistadors use cruel methods, such as dogs, on the native Indians of South America (above).

● c. 1570: the Portuguese set up sugar plantations in Brazil.
● 1585: Sir Walter Raleigh, an Englishman, attempts to

set up an English colony at Roanoke Island (North Carolina), but fails. The settlement does not have adequate resources.

● 1608: Samuel de Champlain founds a French colony at Quebec in Canada.
● 1625: the Dutch establish their North American

In Central and South America the great empires of the Aztecs and the Incas are destroyed by the Spanish in their quest for gold and silver. Toward the end of the 16th century the interest of the Europeans switches northward into North America.

Europe is swept up in a religious quarrel between Catholics and Protestants through the 16th and 17th centuries, with France emerging as Europe's most powerful country. The peoples of the Far East face problems, as European traders move into China and Japan, threatening their traditional ways of life. The fate of the peoples of Africa at the hands of Europeans is bitter, as slave traders take millions of Africans to work in the Caribbean and North America.

1649. Oliver Cromwell takes power as Protector.
● The standard weapon of the time is the musket (below).

● The religious struggle in France is won by the Catholics when, in 1685, King Louis XIV gives French Huguenots the choice of becoming Catholics or leaving the country.
● 1685: the German composer Handel (below) is born. In 1710 he moves to London.

● A new European power, called Prussia, emerges under Frederick William I (1713–40) and his son Frederick the Great (1740–86).
● 1740–48: the War of the Austrian Succession involves the major European countries in a quarrel over who should be Holy Roman Emperor.

● 1714: D. G. Fahrenheit constructs a mercury thermometer with a temperature scale, and is followed by Anders Celsius with his centigrade thermometer in 1742.
● 1733: the invention of the flying shuttle for weaving textiles, by John Kay in Britain, transforms the way goods are made.

● During the 18th century the Ottomans are forced to hand over much territory in Europe to the Austrians and the Russians.

The Ottomans also agree to allow Austria and Russia to protect the interests of the empire's Christian subjects.

● After Suleiman's rule the Ottoman Empire declines, and is threatened by Cossack raiders from the Black Sea.

● 1683: the Ottomans fail to capture Vienna. This brings about a remarkable decline in their power, and the rapid loss of part of their European empire. Hungary has fallen to the forces of the Austrian Habsburgs by the end of the century.

grows. Portugal trades with West African kingdoms for gold, ivory, pepper and cloth, in exchange for goods of little use to the Africans.
● The Dutch and English set up West African trading companies, and the Dutch force Portuguese merchants out of the Gold Coast (now Ghana).

● 1652: the Dutch East India Company founds Cape Town as a base for supplying their trade with the East Indies.
● New states and empires appear in West Africa: the Oyo in Nigeria and the Asante in modern Ghana.
● 1686: the French occupy the island of Madagascar.
● 1687: the first French

Protestants settle at the Cape of Good Hope.
● This head (below) is typical of the work of Benin sculptors.

● The Asante Empire grows rich from trade in slaves, gold and cola nuts.
● The Lunda kingdoms of the Kasai region (Congo basin) also emerge.
● 1749: a Frenchman is the first European to describe the baobab tree (above), while exploring.

● 1644: in China the Ming dynasty is overthrown by the Manchus from the north. The last Ming emperor commits suicide.

● 1664: the French set up their own East India trading company.
● 1674: the Marathas defeat the Mughals.

● The English lose the struggle with the Dutch to control the spice trade of the East Indies, and turn their attention to India. By 1700 they have sole trading rights with key ports such as Calcutta, Bombay and Madras.
● In China the Qing dynasty grows rich from trade with Europe.

● The influence of the Japanese Samurai began to decline in the early 1700s. This steel arrowhead (below) is more decorative than functional.

● Two wars, in 1702–13 and 1744–48, take place between Britain and France, for control of parts of North America and Canada. As a result, Britain acquires Nova Scotia and Newfoundland.
● 1733: New Georgia is settled by British colonists. By the end of this period England's 13 colonies in

capital at the mouth of the Hudson River, on the island of Manhattan. They name it New Amsterdam (above).

● The European struggle to dominate North and South America leads to several conflicts between countries.

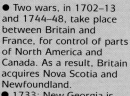

● 1681: William Penn (above), a British Quaker, founds the colony of Pennsylvania in North America.

North America have a population of some 500,000, and a prosperous fur, timber and fishing economy.

PORTUGUESE AND SPANISH EMPIRES

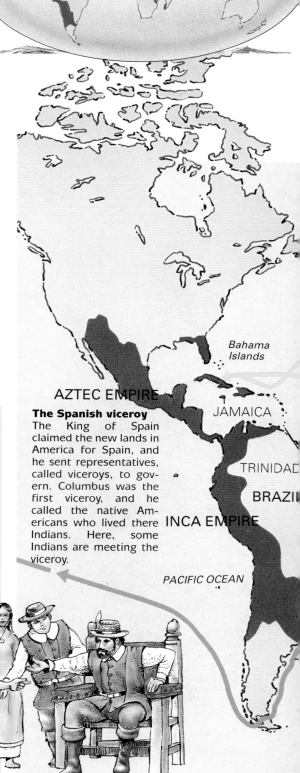

FROM ABOUT 1450, Europeans began a series of voyages of exploration by sea, mainly for the purpose of trade. For centuries Europeans had been trading with China, India and Asia, but they had always traveled on land. In 1453 the Ottoman Turks captured Constantinople (now Istanbul), and blocked their routes. So the Europeans had to find a way of reaching the east by sea. They were also keen to discover more lands. Portugal was one of the leaders in exploration. In the 1460s Portuguese sailors raided the west coast of Africa, looking for gold and slaves. In 1488 Bartholomew Dias sailed to the Cape of Good Hope; in 1498 Vasco da Gama reached India. From then on Portugal set up trading centers around the Indian Ocean. Spain was the other leader in exploration, heading westward. In 1499 Amerigo Vespucci landed on the coast of South America. This unknown continent was named after him. From then on Spanish adventurers conquered territories in the Americas for the king of Spain.

Columbus

Christopher Columbus was an Italian who was given money by King Ferdinand and Queen Isabella of Spain to find a new route to the Far East. He sailed west from Spain, across the Atlantic Ocean. In 1492 he found some islands. Convinced they were Indian islands, he called them the West Indies. In fact, these were the Bahamas, part of the huge American continent. He later found Jamaica, Trinidad and the coast of South America. Columbus remained convinced that he had reached Asia. Columbus died in 1506.

The Spanish viceroy

The King of Spain claimed the new lands in America for Spain, and he sent representatives, called viceroys, to govern. Columbus was the first viceroy, and he called the native Americans who lived there Indians. Here, some Indians are meeting the viceroy.

Bahama Islands

AZTEC EMPIRE

JAMAICA

TRINIDAD

BRAZIL

INCA EMPIRE

PACIFIC OCEAN

Cortes and the Aztecs
When Cortes and his 600 men arrived in the Aztec Empire, they were treated as gods and given gifts. Soon, however, Cortes began conquering the empire. He had guns and horses, which the Aztecs had never seen before, and the conquest took only two years. The Spanish made slaves of the native peoples, and many of them died working in gold and silver mines. Many more died from diseases, such as measles, which the Spanish brought with them from Europe.

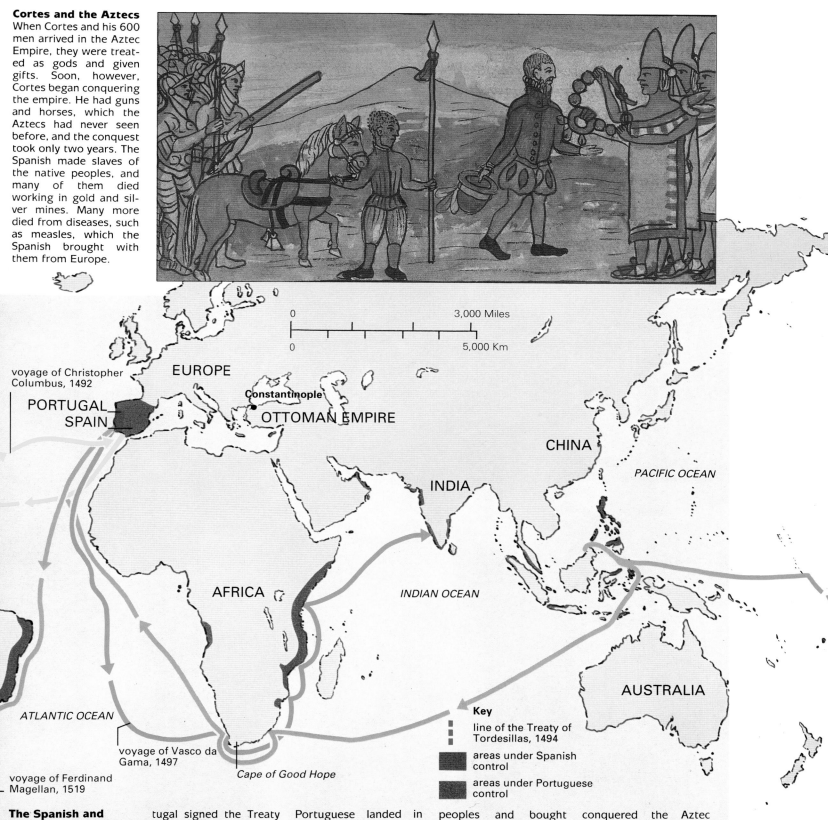

0   3,000 Miles

0   5,000 Km

voice of Christopher
Columbus, 1492

EUROPE

Constantinople

PORTUGAL
SPAIN

OTTOMAN EMPIRE

CHINA

INDIA

PACIFIC OCEAN

AFRICA

INDIAN OCEAN

ATLANTIC OCEAN

voyage of Vasco da
Gama, 1497

Cape of Good Hope

voyage of Ferdinand
Magellan, 1519

AUSTRALIA

Key

line of the Treaty of
Tordesillas, 1494

areas under Spanish
control

areas under Portuguese
control

The Spanish and Portuguese empires in 1580

Soon after the voyages of exploration and discovery started, Spain began to fear that the Portuguese might invade its new territories. In 1494 Spain and Por- | tugal signed the Treaty of Tordesillas, which drew an imaginary line down the "New World." Lands to the east of it went to Portugal, lands to the west, to Spain.

Both Spain and Portugal founded empires out of their new lands. The | Portuguese landed in South America in 1500, east of the line of Tordesillas, and called the new land Brazil. They also set up trading stations in the Indian Ocean and beyond. The Portuguese tried to live alongside the native | peoples and bought goods from them to sell in Portugal. The Spanish, on the other hand, imposed strict control over the lands they conquered in South America.

Between 1519 and 1521 Hernán Cortes | conquered the Aztec Empire, and in the 1530s Francisco Pizarro conquered the Inca Empire. In 1519 a Portuguese sailor, Ferdinand Magellan, began a two-year voyage circling the globe. The journey proved the world was round.

53

RELIGION AND DEVELOPMENT IN EUROPE

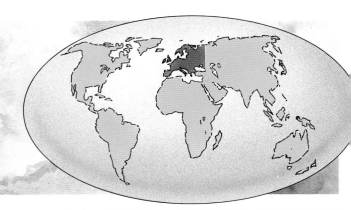

DURING THE 16th and 17th centuries there were great changes in Europe. These influenced the religious, commercial and scientific development of the continent. Several Christian thinkers challenged some beliefs and customs of the Catholic Church. They found supporters in Germany, Scandinavia and England, and a new form of Christianity, called Protestantism, emerged. Its followers were called Protestants because they protested against the Catholic Church. Sometimes violent conflict broke out between Catholics and Protestants. The Thirty Years War (1618–48) began as a religious war in central Europe, and later involved most European countries. This was also a time of important developments in our understanding of the human body, medicine and astronomy. Everywhere it seemed new ideas were changing old ones. Even the power of kings was questioned. In Britain this led to a civil war and the execution of King Charles I.

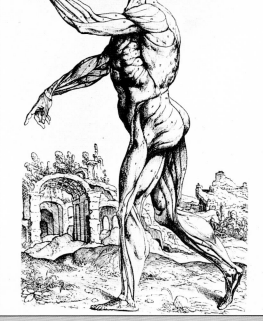

Amsterdam market
Amsterdam was the richest and largest city of the Dutch Republic (now the Netherlands). It is a good example of commercial growth in Europe at this time. The Dutch created great wealth by trading with northern Europe, Asia and the Americas. One reason for their success was the business skills of the Jews who had come to live there. The Jews had been expelled from Catholic Spain and Portugal because of their religion, at the end of the 15th century.

Vesalius and human anatomy
Andreas Vesalius was a 16th-century doctor. He was determined to learn more about human anatomy, or how the body works. By cutting open the bodies of executed criminals he made important discoveries. His drawing of human muscles (above) was published in 1543.

Martin Luther
The most influential of Protestant thinkers and teachers were Martin Luther (1483–1546) and John Calvin (1509–64). Luther lived in Germany where he preached. His ideas spread quickly but they also angered the Roman Catholic Church and its leader, the Pope. Luther criticized the Catholic Church for its elaborate ceremonies, and he said that simple prayers and worship should be based only on the Bible's teachings.

Europe in 1648

The Thirty Years War ended in 1648. The war had been a struggle for power between the kings of France and the Habsburg rulers of the Holy Roman Empire and Spain. It began as a religious war between Protestants and Catholics in 1618, but then became more complicated as other countries, such as Sweden and France, joined in. The Treaty of Westphalia ended the war. The war had brought ruin to Germany and left it divided into 300 separate states. The war also increased the power of a Protestant country, Sweden, and a Catholic country, France. Over the next 50 years France became the most powerful country in Europe.

Louis XIV at Versailles

The leading ruler of Europe after the Thirty Years War was Louis XIV, King of France (1643-1715). Louis built the enormous palace of Versailles, near Paris, to show how powerful and rich he was. He used 36,000 men to build Versailles, and 2,000 people lived there. He surrounded it with vast gardens and a park, containing 1,500 fountains. Louis XIV's absolute style of ruling brought problems for a successor, Louis XVI (1774–1793).

Key

extent of the Holy Roman Empire

0   500 Miles

0   800 Km

NORWAY

SWEDEN

• Stockholm

RUSSIA

DENMARK

• Copenhagen

GREAT BRITAIN

London •

Amsterdam •

DUTCH REPUBLIC

• Berlin

POLAND

• Warsaw

HOLY ROMAN EMPIRE

• Prague

• Paris

FRANCE

SWISS CONFEDERATION

SAVOY

• Milan

• Venice

• Genoa

OTTOMAN EMPIRE

SPAIN

PORTUGAL

• Madrid

• Florence

PAPAL STATES

CORSICA

Rome •

• Lisbon

• Constantinople

• Naples

NAPLES

NORTH AFRICA

SARDINIA

SICILY

• Athens

CRETE

CYPRUS

THE EXPANSION OF RUSSIA

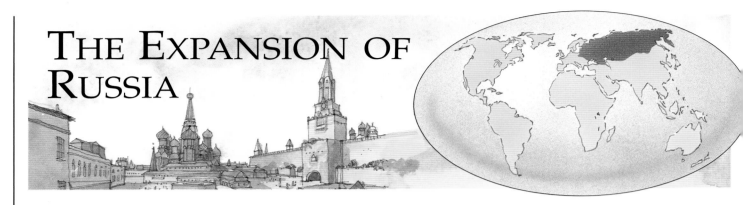

RUSSIA HAD BEEN a Viking and Slav kingdom in the 9th century, with Kiev as its capital. It became Christian at the end of the 10th century, and in the 12th century broke up into smaller princedoms. These were seized in 1240 by the Mongols, who dominated Russia for the next 250 years, isolating it from Europe, and making the people pay taxes. In the 15th century, however, the princedom of Moscovy grew increasingly powerful. Its capital was Moscow. Prince Ivan III of Moscow (1462–1505) stopped paying taxes to the Mongols. Later, Ivan IV (1533–84), known as "Ivan the Terrible," defeated the Mongols in battle. He was crowned tsar (emperor) of Russia in 1547. Ivan the Terrible and the tsars who came after him extended Russian territory, so that by the mid-19th century the Russian Empire stretched from Europe in the west to the Pacific Ocean in the east.

Peter the Great

Peter the Great (1682-1725) was one of the greatest and most effective tsars of Russia. He was the first to try to westernize his country and to make Russia a great power in Europe. He visited Europe, and brought home skills and ideas which he introduced in Russia. For example, he reformed the education and legal systems, and began new industries. He also insisted that Russians dress in European rather than Russian style, and that the men shave off their beards.

St. Petersburg

Peter the Great wanted to establish a Russian seaport, to give him access to Europe. He extended his country to the Baltic Sea, built a powerful navy and captured the delta of the River Neva. Here, at the western edge of the country, he founded a city, naming it St. Petersburg after himself. He made it the capital of Russia. He brought architects from all over Europe to make it a grand and beautiful city in the style of the great cities of Europe. But the site was swampy, and over 150,000 men died building it.

The Winter Palace (above) was built by Peter the Great's daughter, Elizabeth, who ruled after him. It became the royal family home.

Russia's colonization of Siberia

Siberia is a huge area of northern Asia between the Ural Mountains and the Pacific Ocean. It extends for over 3,500 miles. Most of Siberia is poor land covered by thick forest, called taiga. The trees of the taiga are conifers, such as pines and firs. The land in southern Siberia is better for growing crops.

Between 1580 and 1649 Russians explored Siberia and claimed it for Russia. They established forts at important places and gradually towns grew up around the forts. The population of Siberia has always been small because of the poor land and extremely cold winters. In 1700 there were only about 200,000 Russian settlers living there.

Russian expansion

The expansion of Russia began in the 15th century. At that time the rulers of Moscow started to reunite the lands around Moscow which were ruled by Russians.

In the 16th century Ivan the Terrible began to extend Russia to the east. The power of Poland and Sweden made expansion into Europe difficult, but by 1667 Russia conquered lands on the eastern side of the River Dnieper, including the city of Kiev.

From 1580 the Russian army moved east, over the Ural Mountains and into Siberia, where they took land very quickly. By 1620 they had reached the Yenisei River, in central Siberia. In 1649 they established the town of Okhotsk on the Pacific coast.

In the late 18th century Russia occupied Alaska, but in 1867 Tsar Alexander II sold it to the United States of America for 7 million dollars – just two cents an acre! This brought the east coast of Russia to within 62 miles of its future rival, the USA.

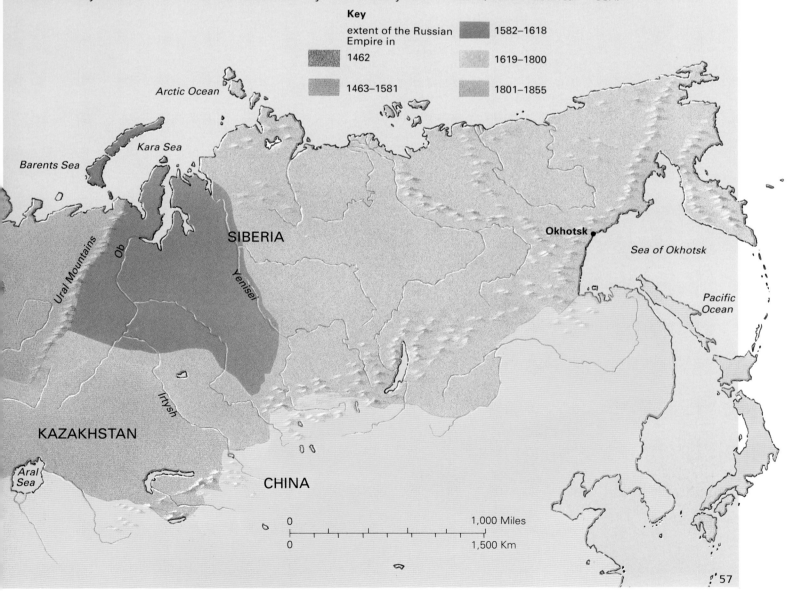

Key

extent of the Russian Empire in

- 1462
- 1463–1581
- 1582–1618
- 1619–1800
- 1801–1855

Arctic Ocean

Barents Sea

Kara Sea

SIBERIA

Ural Mountains

Ob

Yenisei

Irtysh

KAZAKHSTAN

Aral Sea

CHINA

Okhotsk

Sea of Okhotsk

Pacific Ocean

| 0 | | 1,000 Miles |
| 0 | | 1,500 Km |

NEW ISLAMIC EMPIRES

THE FIRST ISLAMIC empire, set up in the 7th and 8th centuries, gradually broke up. The Mongols captured its capital, Baghdad, in 1258 (see page 44). From the 14th to the 16th centuries three new Islamic empires appeared, so that by 1600 the Islamic world was far larger than the Christian world. The first was the Ottoman Empire. It was created by Turks in western Anatolia (modern Turkey) in the early 14th century. It had a fine army. Ottoman soldiers believed it was their Islamic duty to defeat the Christian infidels (nonbelievers). For them, death in battle was an honor. By the mid-16th century the empire ruled over 25 million people, from Turks and Greeks to Persians and Arabs. It survived until the early 20th century. The second Islamic empire of this period was the Safavid Empire which conquered all of Persia and parts of Iran. It lasted from 1501–1732. The third was the Mughal Empire in India. It was founded in the 16th century in northern India by the ruler Babur, and then expanded into the south. It lasted for about 200 years.

Janissary soldiers
Much of the Ottoman Empire's success was due to its army, which was large and highly trained. Most of the troops were part-time cavalry, but there was an elite group of full-time foot soldiers called Janissaries. They were Christians who had been captured or recruited from Europe, some taken when they were still young boys.

HOLY ROMAN EMPIRE

FRANCE   Venice

SPAIN   Rome

ITALY

Mediterranean Sea

TUNISIA

ALGERIA

Ottoman Turks besiege Vienna
From the 14th century onward, the Ottoman emperors were determined to expand into Europe, through the Balkans. Twice the Ottoman army attacked Vienna, the capital city of the Holy Roman Empire, which blocked the way to further advances. In the autumn of 1529 the Emperor Suleiman besieged the city for three weeks. He had large forces and cannons, but the Viennese defenders held out. Suleiman was forced to withdraw in October, because he was anxious to return home before the winter set in. The Ottomans attacked Vienna again in 1683, but they failed once again after a siege that lasted for eight weeks.

0		1,000 Miles
0		1,500 Km

58

The Taj Mahal

The early Mughal emperors built many splendid buildings. One of the most beautiful is the Taj Mahal in India. It was built by Emperor Shah Jahan (1592-1666) as a tomb for his favorite wife, Mumtaz Mahal, who died in 1631. The main building (right) took 11 years to build and 20,000 men worked on it. The building is covered in white marble, which reflects the changing colors of the sun. Like all Mughal tombs, the Taj Mahal stands in a designed garden.

The expansion of the Ottoman Empire

At its height in the mid-16th century, the Ottoman Empire was one of the most successful empires in the world. It began in Anatolia (modern Turkey) and expanded into Europe, Asia and Africa. The capture of Constantinople in 1453 was its greatest prize. The Ottomans renamed the city Istanbul and made it the capital of their empire. Selim I (1512–20) added Muslim lands of the Middle East – Syria, Egypt, Algeria and the holy cities of Mecca and Medina – to the empire. His successor, Suleiman I (1520–66), known as Suleiman the Magnificent, conquered more land in North Africa, Iraq and Europe. After Suleiman there were no more great conquests. By the time of his death, the Ottomans were at war with the neighboring Safavid Empire in Persia (now Iran). The Muslims who lived here belonged to a different sect, or group, and the two empires fought over their religious differences.

The expansion of the Mughal Empire

The Mughal Empire was founded in 1526 by a Muslim, Babur. He was a descendant of the Mongol leader, Chinghiz Khan (see page 44). He had set up a kingdom in Afghanistan and tried to capture more land to the north, but failed. He then turned his attention to northern India, where there was no strong ruler to oppose him. Between 1526 and 1530 he conquered much of northern India. He made Delhi his capital. His descendants added more Indian land to the empire, but many of the coastal towns were occupied by Europeans seeking trade (see page 52). In the 18th century rival groups weakened the empire.

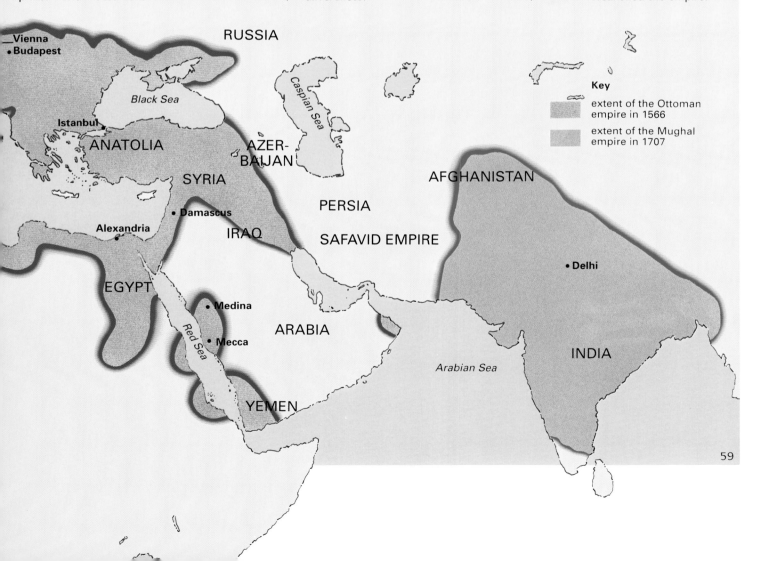

RUSSIA

Vienna
Budapest

Black Sea

Caspian Sea

Istanbul

ANATOLIA

AZER-
BAIJAN

AFGHANISTAN

SYRIA

PERSIA

Damascus

Alexandria

IRAQ

SAFAVID EMPIRE

Delhi

EGYPT

Medina

Red Sea

ARABIA

Mecca

INDIA

Arabian Sea

YEMEN

Key

extent of the Ottoman empire in 1566

extent of the Mughal empire in 1707

THE EXPANSION OF CHINA

IN THE 13th CENTURY Mongols from the north conquered China (see page 44). The Mongol leader Qubilai Khan (Kublai Khan) founded the Yuan dynasty of emperors. In 1388 the Mongols were overthrown and a new Chinese dynasty, the Ming, began to rule. They were in power for nearly 300 years, until 1644. At first the Ming emperors made China the richest and most organized country in the world. They kept the vast country peaceful and attacked their neighbors. They also rebuilt the Great Wall in stone, to strengthen it against invaders. But when they asked the Chinese people, whose harvests were poor, to pay higher taxes, the people rebelled. This weakened the country, and made it easier for outsiders to attack. In 1644 the Manchus invaded China from Manchuria in the northeast. The Ming emperor killed himself, and the Manchu leader set himself up as the new emperor of China. His dynasty, the Qing, ruled China until 1911.

A Chinese examination

From the 7th century Chinese emperors chose their advisers and officials by making them take exams. They were tested on the writings of the Chinese thinker, Confucius, and his followers. Confucius had lived in the 6th and 5th centuries BC, but his teachings on how to encourage peace and order in society had been adopted as the official philosophy of the Chinese Empire and were still thought of as very important. This painting shows county magistrates taking an exam. It was painted in the 18th century.

Xinjiang Province

In the 18th century the Qing emperors increased the territory of the Chinese Empire. They extended their rule over the neighboring kingdoms to the north and west. Xinjiang Province lies in the far northwest of China, a very long way from Beijing. It was only officially made a province of China in 1884. Xinjiang means "New Region."

Christianity in China

In 1583 Mateo Ricci, a Catholic Christian from Europe, entered China. He lived at the imperial court in Beijing and encouraged the Chinese to become Christians. He is seen here (on the left) with an important Chinese whom he has converted. By 1650, 150,000 Chinese had converted to Christianity.

Ming porcelain
Throughout its history China has made high-quality pottery, or porcelain. In the Ming period potters made splendid blue-and-white ware, like this vase. Some pots were exported to Europe, where they were greatly valued. The Europeans called them china.

The Forbidden City
Qubilai Khan rebuilt the city of Beijing in 1261. At its heart is the Forbidden City, containing the palace of the emperor and his family, temples and gardens. It was forbidden for anyone but the emperor and his officials to enter it. Beijing is halfway between China and Mongolia, so from there the Mongol emperors could control both countries. In 1421 it became the capital of China, and is the capital today. It was again rebuilt during the Ming dynasty.

Key

original Manchu homeland

extent of Manchu expansion to 1644

expansion 1645–1659

expansion 1659–1760

extent of the Chinese Empire in 1760

Expansion of the Chinese Empire
For 40 years after the beginning of the Qing dynasty, Chinese rebels fought the new emperors. Eventually the Qing emperors won. They strengthened the state and began to extend their territory to the north and west. They added Mongolia, Tibet, and Sinkiang to the Chinese Empire. The empire was now more than twice its earlier size. The Qing emperors also set up trading links with Europe. They exported porcelain, tea, cotton and silk, and imported gold and silver. But they did not allow the culture of Europe to influence Chinese culture. They were proud of their own culture and remained independent.

MANCHURIA

MONGOLIA

XINJIANG

SINKIANG

Beijing

KOREA

Yellow Sea

TIBET

NEPAL

TAIWAN

0   800 Miles

0   1,200 Km

BURMA

SIAM   LAOS

JAPAN IN WAR AND PEACE

THE KINGDOM OF Japan was created in the 3rd century AD by the ancestors of the present emperor. At the end of the 7th century, the emperor divided the country into provinces, each ruled by an officer. Although the emperor was the official ruler, real power was held by the most powerful warrior lord in Japan, the "shogun." In the 15th century the warrior families fought each other, destroying the countryside and disrupting Japanese life. In 1603, though, the shogun Ieyasu Tokugawa united the country and brought it peace. The Tokugawa family ruled Japan with a strong government for over 250 years. Like China, Japan did not have much contact with Europe. In 1542, however, the first Portuguese trading ships reached Japan. They were followed by Christian missionaries, who came to convert the Japanese from their Buddhist and Shinto religions to Christianity. The shogun felt threatened. He expelled the missionaries and put to death all Japanese Christians. He also stopped almost all trade with Europe. This isolated Japan until the mid-19th century.

Japanese towns and cities
This painting shows Nijo castle and the busy streets of its nearby town. In the 15th and 16th centuries many Japanese lords built castles for themselves and their samurai followers. Often, as at Nijo, towns grew up around these castles. Other towns grew up around Buddhist monasteries. However, most Japanese lived in villages. These usually belonged to the emperor, to monasteries or to local lords.

Japanese Kabuki
The Japanese have developed several different kinds of theater. The most popular is Kabuki, which means "song, dance, skill." All the characters are played by men, wearing colorful clothes. The other kinds of Japanese theater are Noh, in which the actors wear masks, and Bunraku, which uses puppets.

A samurai warrior
Each local lord had his own force of warriors called samurai. The loyalty of these samurai to their lord was total. They preferred to die rather than to dishonor their lord. Samurai wore heavy, elaborate armor and they fought on horseback.

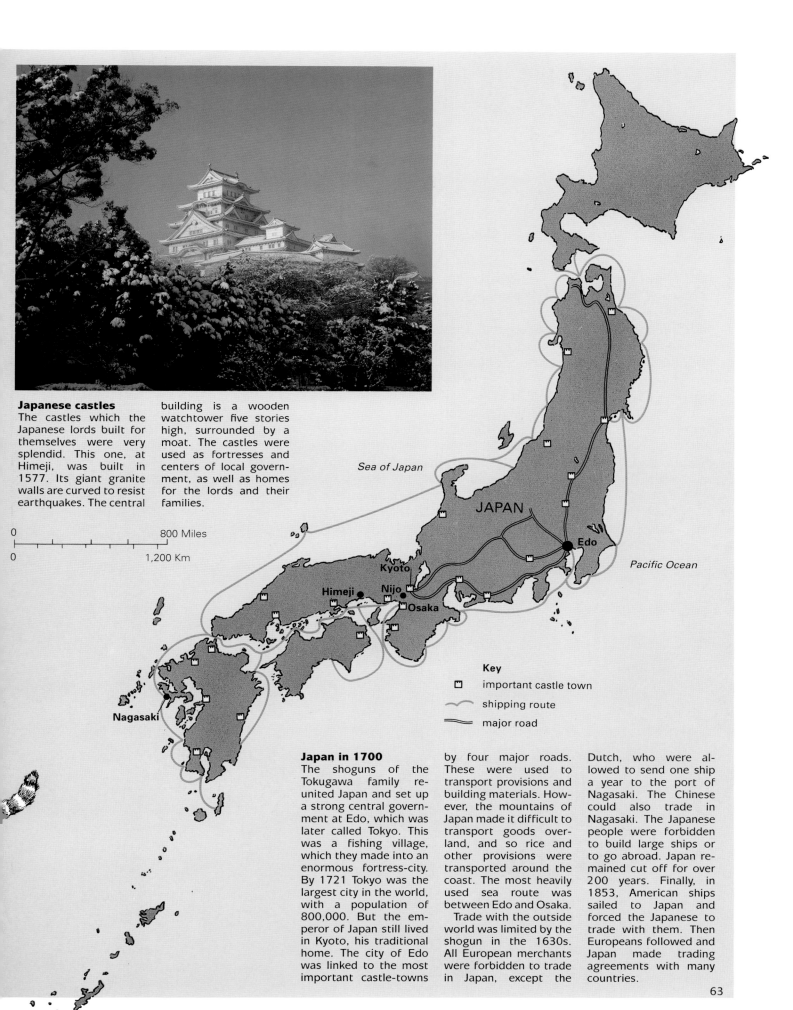

Japanese castles

The castles which the Japanese lords built for themselves were very splendid. This one, at Himeji, was built in 1577. Its giant granite walls are curved to resist earthquakes. The central building is a wooden watchtower five stories high, surrounded by a moat. The castles were used as fortresses and centers of local government, as well as homes for the lords and their families.

0 ————————— 800 Miles

0 ————————— 1,200 Km

Sea of Japan

JAPAN

Edo

Pacific Ocean

Kyoto

Himeji   Nijo

Osaka

Nagasaki

Key

◻ important castle town

⌒ shipping route

═ major road

Japan in 1700

The shoguns of the Tokugawa family re-united Japan and set up a strong central government at Edo, which was later called Tokyo. This was a fishing village, which they made into an enormous fortress-city. By 1721 Tokyo was the largest city in the world, with a population of 800,000. But the emperor of Japan still lived in Kyoto, his traditional home. The city of Edo was linked to the most important castle-towns by four major roads. These were used to transport provisions and building materials. However, the mountains of Japan made it difficult to transport goods overland, and so rice and other provisions were transported around the coast. The most heavily used sea route was between Edo and Osaka.

Trade with the outside world was limited by the shogun in the 1630s. All European merchants were forbidden to trade in Japan, except the Dutch, who were allowed to send one ship a year to the port of Nagasaki. The Chinese could also trade in Nagasaki. The Japanese people were forbidden to build large ships or to go abroad. Japan remained cut off for over 200 years. Finally, in 1853, American ships sailed to Japan and forced the Japanese to trade with them. Then Europeans followed and Japan made trading agreements with many countries.

EUROPEANS IN ASIA AND THE PACIFIC

IN 1498 THE PORTUGUESE sailor Vasco da Gama reached India by sea (see page 52). The discovery of this new route gave the Portuguese important trading advantages. By 1550 they controlled trade in the Indian Ocean and in the Spice Islands in the East Indies (now Indonesia). Portugal remained the main European power trading with Asia for almost a century. But in the 17th century Dutch, British and French companies began to compete with the Portuguese for this valuable trade – especially in spices, gold and silver. The Dutch were a rich trading nation. They drove the Portuguese out of the Spice Islands and set up a vast empire in southeast Asia. Britain, too, was a great sea power. Like the Dutch, the British set up an East India Company to organize trade in Asia. When the Dutch forced them out of the Spice Islands the British turned to India, where they traded in cotton, silk and spices. In the 18th century they fought the French, who had also established trade links with India.

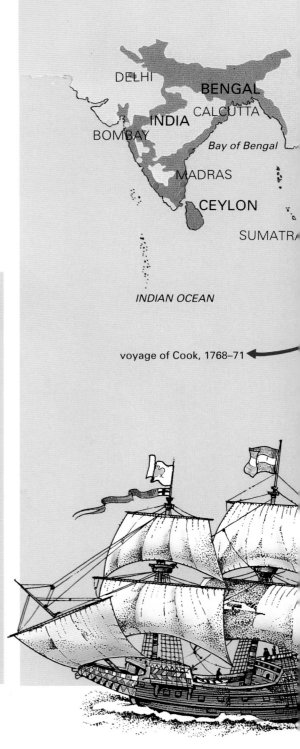

DELHI

BENGAL

CALCUTTA

INDIA

BOMBAY

Bay of Bengal

MADRAS

CEYLON

SUMATRA

INDIAN OCEAN

voyage of Cook, 1768–71

The British in India
This painting shows a British official in India at a music party. In the 17th century the East India Company built trading stations at Bombay, Madras and Calcutta. At first the Mughal emperors of India allowed this, but in 1756 the local ruler of Bengal, the nawab, attacked the British at Calcutta. The British won and were given the right to govern Bengal. By 1800 Britain had made treaties with other local rulers, and had become the leading power in India.

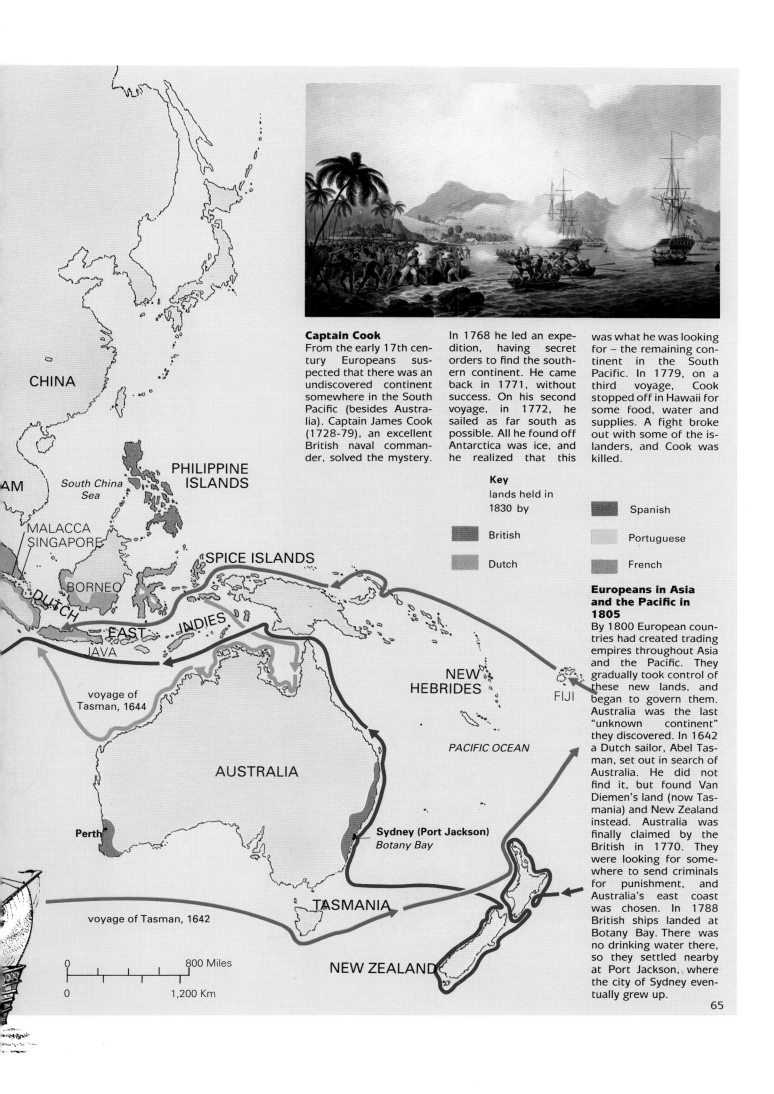

CHINA

PHILIPPINE
ISLANDS

*South China
Sea*

MALACCA
SINGAPORE

AM

SPICE ISLANDS

BORNEO

DUTCH

EAST INDIES

JAVA

*voyage of
Tasman, 1644*

NEW
HEBRIDES

FIJI

PACIFIC OCEAN

AUSTRALIA

Perth

Sydney (Port Jackson)
Botany Bay

voyage of Tasman, 1642

TASMANIA

NEW ZEALAND

0   800 Miles

0   1,200 Km

Captain Cook

From the early 17th century Europeans suspected that there was an undiscovered continent somewhere in the South Pacific (besides Australia). Captain James Cook (1728-79), an excellent British naval commander, solved the mystery.

In 1768 he led an expedition, having secret orders to find the southern continent. He came back in 1771, without success. On his second voyage, in 1772, he sailed as far south as possible. All he found off Antarctica was ice, and he realized that this

was what he was looking for – the remaining continent in the South Pacific. In 1779, on a third voyage, Cook stopped off in Hawaii for some food, water and supplies. A fight broke out with some of the islanders, and Cook was killed.

Key
lands held in
1830 by

British

Dutch

Spanish

Portuguese

French

Europeans in Asia and the Pacific in 1805

By 1800 European countries had created trading empires throughout Asia and the Pacific. They gradually took control of these new lands, and began to govern them. Australia was the last "unknown continent" they discovered. In 1642 a Dutch sailor, Abel Tasman, set out in search of Australia. He did not find it, but found Van Diemen's land (now Tasmania) and New Zealand instead. Australia was finally claimed by the British in 1770. They were looking for somewhere to send criminals for punishment, and Australia's east coast was chosen. In 1788 British ships landed at Botany Bay. There was no drinking water there, so they settled nearby at Port Jackson, where the city of Sydney eventually grew up.

65

INDUSTRY AND REVOLUTION

The French and American Revolutions, and colonization in Africa and Asia. The Industrial Revolution transforms Europe.

EUROPE

- Prussia and Russia emerge as major European powers.
- 1789: the French Revolution begins. Citizens protest for "Liberty or Death" (right). France is declared a republic in 1792 and King Louis XVI is executed.

- War breaks out in Europe in 1792.
- The Industrial Revolution begins in Britain.

- France creates a vast empire in Europe under Emperor Napoleon.
- 1814: Louis XVIII, brother of the executed Louis XVI, becomes king as the monarchy in France is restored.
- 1815: Napoleon is finally defeated at the battle of Waterloo.
- 1824: Charles X becomes King of France.

- Metternich, Chancellor of the Austrian Empire, tries to stop the spread of any revolutionary ideas in Europe.
- 1848: revolutions occur in France and Europe's main cities.

MIDDLE EAST

- 1792: the Treaty of Jassy ends a long war between the Ottoman Empire, and Russia and the Habsburg Empire. The Turks surrender Hungary, which the Habsburgs begin to resettle. The decline of Ottoman power in the Middle East makes Britain worry about Russia's attempts to increase its own power.

- 1820: Britain establishes control in the states around the Persian Gulf, such as Oman.

- Mohammed Ali, sent to restore Ottoman control of Egypt, founds his own dynasty there.

- 1826: the Ottoman janissaries (above) are wiped out in a massacre by sultan Mahmud II.

AFRICA

- 1755: an outbreak of smallpox in Cape Town kills many Africans.
- European settlers in South Africa begin the first of many wars of expansion to the north and east of Cape Colony.
- 1787: Freetown, in Sierra Leone, is founded as a home for Africans freed from slavery.
- 1798: Mungo Park, a Scottish explorer, reaches Niger.
- 1798: Napoleon Bonaparte invades Egypt in his war against Britain.

- 1807: Britain outlaws slave trading by British citizens.
- By 1811 the Fulani people have completed their conquest of the Hausa kingdoms of northern Nigeria.
- 1815: the Dutch surrender Cape Colony to the British.

- The Zulu warrior Shaka (above) creates the Zulu kingdom in southern Africa.

- In East Africa a new slave trade emerges, run by Arabs from Zanzibar and the Portuguese.
- 1836: the Great Trek of Afrikaners (whites of Dutch descent) begins as they leave Cape Colony to escape British control.

- The Tuaregs (above), who live in the Sahel desert region, are hostile to Europeans.

ASIA AND AUSTRALASIA

- Captain James Cook explores the South Pacific and proves that there is no unknown South Pacific continent. Below, he is shown hunting walruses off Alaska on his third voyage.

- China under the Qing dynasty is the world's largest empire with the biggest population. It has control over much of southeast Asia, including Korea, Siam, Burma and Nepal.

- The Chinese economy weakens as it begins to import more opium than it exports tea and silk.
- 1839–42: the Opium Wars in China against Britain, to stop the illegal opium trade. The Chinese lose and surrender Hong Kong to Britain.
- 1840: Maori chiefs sign their lands over to the Crown (below).

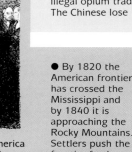

NORTH AND SOUTH AMERICA

- 1763: Britain wins control of Canada.
- 1776: the American colonies declare independence from British rule (right).
- 1789: George Washington is the first President of the USA.

- 1808: a law is passed in the United States banning the import of slaves.
- 1810–26: in South and Central America the colonies win their independence from the Spanish and Portuguese.

- By 1820 the American frontier has crossed the Mississippi and by 1840 it is approaching the Rocky Mountains. Settlers push the frontier further west as they search for rich farmland. The native American Indians, such as the Cherokees in 1838, are driven out of their traditional lands.

1750   1800   1825

The United States wins its independence from Britain and expands its territory across North America, defeating the Native Indian population.

Africa attracts the attention first of European explorers and then of European armies, as most of the continent is seized by powers keen to extend their empires.

In Europe, revolution in France in 1789 generates ideas which bring about the creation of two major European nations, Italy and Germany. The Industrial Revolution, begun in Britain, spreads across Europe, transforming it with factories and new methods of making goods.

China is not spared the interest of the European powers as Britain, France and Germany try to control parts of it.

● Piedmont (below) drives Austria out of northern Italy, and by 1870 unifies the various states in the Kingdom of Italy.
● 1871: Bismarck, Chancellor of Prussia, creates a united Germany.

● Germany becomes Europe's strongest economic power and begins expanding its army and navy to challenge Britain.
● A period of reform in Russia under Alexander II (1855–81) is replaced by one of conservatism as his son, Alexander III, and grandson, Nicholas II, undo much of his work.

● 1909: Louis Blériot (below) is the first person to fly across the English Channel.

● The tension in Europe increases. Britain allies with France and Russia against Germany.

● The rulers of the Ottoman Empire try to prevent further decline by reforming and modernizing their lands. They declare freedom of worship and a fairer taxation system.

● Muhammad Ahmad's tomb (above). He is successor of the Prophet.

● The Ottoman ruler Abdul Hamid II (1876–1909) faces opposition from his Arab provinces. The empire is reduced to Turkey, a small corner of southeast Europe, and the Arab provinces of Asia.

● 1909: the Young Turks (left) overthrow Abdul Hamid in a campaign for more freedoms.

● 1857: Speke, from Britain, begins his first expedition to find the source of the Nile, but many people do not believe his claim to have found it (Lake Victoria).
● A Dutch woman explorer, Tinne, also attempts to find the source of the Nile but is killed by Tuaregs as she crosses the Libyan desert in 1863.
● 1867: diamonds are discovered in South Africa.
● 1874: the British establish the Gold Coast colony (now Ghana).

● 1896: Ethiopia is liberated from Italian rule. The Ethiopian emperor Menelik (below). begins to modernize his country.
● 1875–1900: the "Scramble for Africa" among Europeans.

● 1899–1902: the Boer War between the Afrikaners and the British leaves the Orange Free State and Transvaal in British hands.
● 1908: Belgium seizes the Congo.
● 1910: South Africa becomes an independent state in the British Empire.
● 1912: the French seize Morocco and the Italians seize Libya.

● 1854: Japan opens two ports to US trade.
● 1857: Indian Mutiny against Britain.

● 1858: the British government takes over the running of India from the East India Company.

● Japan begins to modernize and expand, as it acquires territories in the Pacific region. War with China (1894–95) brings it Formosa (Taiwan). This leads to hostility from Russia and war ten years later in 1904.

● 1900: the Boxer Rebellion in China against foreigners.
● 1904–05: Japan wins a startling victory against Russia and acquires more territory in Manchuria.
● 1910: Japan occupies Korea. This increase in Japanese power in southeast Asia worries the United States.
● 1911: the Qing dynasty, which has ruled China since 1644, is overthrown by Sun Yat-sen's democratic Guomindang party. The country is caught up in civil war.

● The southern states continue to keep slaves who were brought across the Atlantic (above).

● 1861–65: the American Civil War, between the southern and northern states.

● The United States becomes a world power as it establishes important bases in the Pacific, including Pearl Harbor and Midway. The US goes to war with Spain in 1898 and takes over the Philippines, Guam and Puerto Rico.

● A US trade union label (above).

● The United States becomes the world's greatest producer of steel, coal and iron
● The US extends its influence throughout the Caribbean and Central America over states such as Cuba, the Dominican Republic, Panama and Nicaragua.
● 1907: the US fleet goes on a world tour, as the United States shows Europe its military power and warns them to keep out of Central and South America.

67

1850   1875   1900   1913

THE INDUSTRIAL REVOLUTION

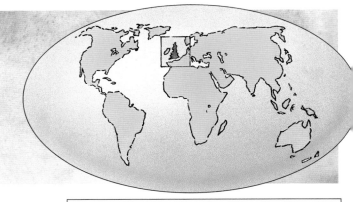

IN THE 18th CENTURY most people throughout the world supported themselves with farming, or agriculture. But in Britain a set of changes began which led to the invention of machines and new ways of processing raw materials. Over the next 100 years Britain changed from being an agricultural country to being an industrial one. This process is known as the Industrial Revolution.

In the early 18th century workers made cloth at home, using simple, hand-powered machines. This was called "cottage industry." Cottage industry started to decline with the introduction of the steam engine, a very important invention of the Industrial Revolution. In 1781 the Scottish engineer James Watt discovered that a steam engine could drive other machines, such as textile-weaving machines. Goods could then be made much more cheaply. Factories grew up all over Britain, where there was plenty of coal to fuel the engines, and it became the industrial center of the world. Soon other European countries followed in the process of industrialization.

THE WHITE SLAVES OF ENGLAND.

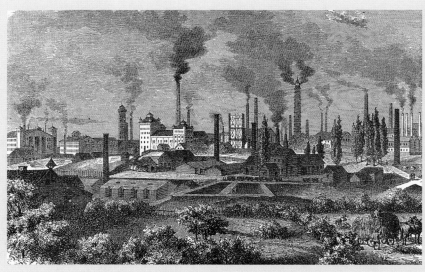

Children at work
Many women and children were used to operate machines in the new factories. The machines did not need skilled workers, and since women and children could be paid less than men they were employed instead. Children, because they were small, could also get to awkward places and repair the machines. They were often hurt and had to work very long hours. If they fell asleep they were fined.

Industrial progress in Germany
From 1870 to 1914 British industrial output doubled, but in the United States it tripled, and in Germany it quadrupled. Industry grew at such a rate in Germany because the country had developed an internal combustion engine that ran on gasoline and could drive machines, cars, and ships. This factory at Essen in the Ruhr Valley opened in 1840 to make weapons from steel. By the 1860s the small village had been transformed into this industrial landscape. In the 1870s the factory was extended even further and houses were built for the workers and their families.

Opening the Stockton and Darlington Railway

The Stockton and Darlington Railway was the world's first successful, steam-powered public railway. It was designed by George Stephenson and opened in 1825. The idea of pulling trucks on rails was not a new one. Horses had been pulling wagons on rails for over 200 years, but most engineers thought a steam-driven wheel could not grip an iron rail. But one man, called Richard Trevithick, was convinced it could. In 1810 he built a steam engine which did just that. Locomotives (engines) were soon pulling wagons filled with coal across northeast England. From this came the idea of using railways to transport people, as well as goods. After the opening of the Stockton and Darlington Railway, more railways were built in Britain and abroad. This changed many people's way of life, as they could travel more easily to different parts of the country.

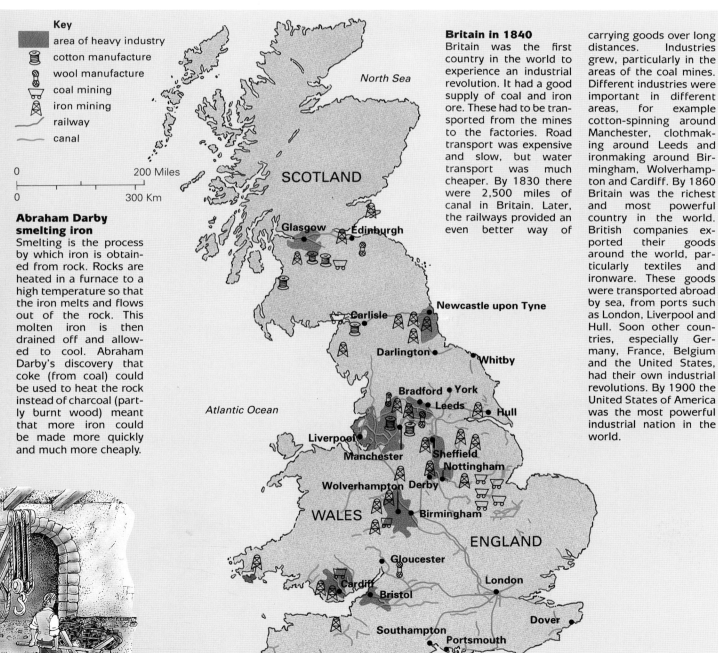

Key

- ▨ area of heavy industry
- cotton manufacture
- wool manufacture
- coal mining
- iron mining
- railway
- canal

0 — 200 Miles
0 — 300 Km

Abraham Darby smelting iron

Smelting is the process by which iron is obtained from rock. Rocks are heated in a furnace to a high temperature so that the iron melts and flows out of the rock. This molten iron is then drained off and allowed to cool. Abraham Darby's discovery that coke (from coal) could be used to heat the rock instead of charcoal (partly burnt wood) meant that more iron could be made more quickly and much more cheaply.

Britain in 1840

Britain was the first country in the world to experience an industrial revolution. It had a good supply of coal and iron ore. These had to be transported from the mines to the factories. Road transport was expensive and slow, but water transport was much cheaper. By 1830 there were 2,500 miles of canal in Britain. Later, the railways provided an even better way of carrying goods over long distances. Industries grew, particularly in the areas of the coal mines. Different industries were important in different areas, for example cotton-spinning around Manchester, clothmaking around Leeds and ironmaking around Birmingham, Wolverhampton and Cardiff. By 1860 Britain was the richest and most powerful country in the world. British companies exported their goods around the world, particularly textiles and ironware. These goods were transported abroad by sea, from ports such as London, Liverpool and Hull. Soon other countries, especially Germany, France, Belgium and the United States, had their own industrial revolutions. By 1900 the United States of America was the most powerful industrial nation in the world.

69

THE FRENCH REVOLUTION

A T THE END OF the 18th century, French society was divided. The king, the nobles and the church had great power, which they could use against the people. The middle classes and the peasants were being heavily taxed, and poor harvests had left many people starving. In 1787 King Louis XVI called the Estates-General, or parliament, to raise yet more taxes, now approaching the nobles for taxes too. The nobles refused, and a financial crisis followed. In 1789 the bourgeoisie (middle class) rose in revolt. They set up their own parliament, the National Assembly, and tried to reform the government. The people of Paris also began rioting in the streets. They attacked the Bastille (the royal prison), and set free all the prisoners. The Revolution soon spread to other parts of France. In 1792 the King was put on trial and executed. France then became a republic (governed by elected representatives). Radical politicians, however, began executing anybody opposed to the Revolution. In 1795 a new government restored some calm, and in 1799 the Revolution ended when Napoleon Bonaparte seized power.

A revolutionary committee

The new government set up revolutionary committees (above) in 1793 to sentence "enemies of the Revolution." The usual sentence was death. One man was executed for simply saying "Long live the King."

Treasure taken from churches

In 1793 revolutionaries seized and sold church valuables (below) to pay for the French army fighting in Europe. Many churches were closed down and this turned many ordinary people against the Revolution.

The execution of Louis XVI

Louis was executed on January 21, 1793. The revolutionaries accused him of betraying France by plotting with foreign rulers to get rid of the revolutionary government. In the same year his wife, Marie Antoin- ette, was also executed. The revolutionaries used a new machine for exe- cuting them, called a guillotine. This had a sharp blade which sliced off the person's head. But in Louis' case, ac- cording to an eyewit- ness, the blade did not do its job as effectively as it should, and the king let out a scream after the blade had fallen. Once his head had been prop- erly severed, the execu- tioner held it up for the crowd to see. More than 40,000 opponents of the Revolution were ex- ecuted between 1789 and 1794.

Napoleon's retreat from Moscow

In June 1812 Napoleon invaded Russia with 500,000 troops, to punish the tsar (emperor) for supporting France's enemies. The Russians retreated and allowed Napoleon to capture a deserted Moscow, set on fire by the Russians themselves. Napoleon's army was forced to begin the long march back to France, through a freezing Russian winter. Tens of thousands died from cold, hunger and sudden attacks by Russian cavalry. Only 50,000 survived.

Europe in 1810

The French revolutionaries were determined to spread the idea of representative government to the other peoples of Europe. By 1793 all Europe was involved in the French Revolution.

The rulers of Europe joined in alliance against France, but the French army, led by Napoleon Bonaparte, was the best in Europe. In 1804 Napoleon had himself crowned Emperor of the French, and by 1810 most of Europe was ruled by France or her allies. Members of Napoleon's family ruled as kings in Spain, Holland, Naples and Westphalia (northern Germany).

There were only two countries Napoleon could not defeat: Britain and Russia. Britain was able to protect itself with its powerful navy. Napoleon's invasion of Russia in 1812 was unsuccessful and his army was badly weakened. Napoleon was forced to give up as ruler of France in 1814 and was sent to the island of Elba as punishment. But in 1815 he escaped and raised another army in France.

Napoleon was finally defeated by Britain and its allies at the Battle of Waterloo. He was exiled to another island, St. Helena, in the Atlantic Ocean, west of Africa. He died there in 1821. His body was brought back to France in 1840.

Key

- extent of Napoleon's French empire in 1810
- ally of Napoleon
- area under Napoleon's control
- independent state

0   500 Miles
0   800 Km

NORWAY
SWEDEN
Moscow
RUSSIAN EMPIRE
DENMARK
GREAT BRITAIN
London
HOLLAND
Amsterdam
PRUSSIA
GRAND DUCHY OF WARSAW
Battle of Waterloo
Paris
CONFEDERATION OF THE RHINE
AUSTRIAN EMPIRE
FRANCE
SWITZERLAND
ILLYRIAN PROVINCE
Black Sea
PORTUGAL
SPAIN
ITALY
OTTOMAN EMPIRE
CORSICA
Madrid
ELBA
Rome
NAPLES
SARDINIA
Mediterranean Sea
SICILY

71

INDEPENDENCE IN LATIN AMERICA

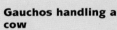

IN THE 16th CENTURY Spain and Portugal conquered large parts of America. Central and South America are called Latin America because the conquerors introduced languages there related to Latin. Latin America was ruled for centuries by officials sent out from Spain and Portugal. Eventually the descendants of the original settlers began to resent this. When the American colonies became independent from Britain in 1783, these Spanish Americans wanted independence too. They were not strong enough to defeat the Spanish rulers then, but events in Europe soon helped them. The French Revolution of 1789 led to the rise of Napoleon and the Napoleonic Wars in Europe (see page 70). When Napoleon invaded Spain some Spanish Americans in Latin America tried to govern themselves. A Spanish army was sent there to restore control in 1814, but a general revolt, and brilliant military campaigns by Simón Bolívar and José de San Martín, forced the Spanish to leave. This led to the creation of the first independent countries of Latin America.

Simón Bolívar

Simón Bolívar was a politician and military leader who believed that the peoples of Latin America had a right to govern themselves. He knew this would mean war with Spain. In 1817 he led an army through the Andes mountains to New Granada, and in 1819 captured the capital, Bogotá, freeing the country from Spanish rule. This triumph was quickly followed by independence for Venezuela, Peru, Bolivia (named after him) and Ecuador. Bolívar wanted South America to become a single country, which would include Chile and Argentina (both freed by José de San Martín). This did not happen, however.

Gauchos handling a cow

Gauchos were horsemen who herded cattle on the vast plains, or pampas, of Argentina, Uruguay and Paraguay in the 18th and 19th centuries. Once a year they drove the cattle into the main towns, where the cattle were slaughtered. A lot of the meat was then exported to Europe.

Railways and progress

Latin America's economic development was partly due to the immigration of people from Europe in the late 19th and early 20th centuries. They organized the building of railways and ports. Railways made it possible to transport goods to their coasts, and from these to North America and Europe. Argentina exported beef, Venezuela coffee, and Peru guano (bird droppings used as manure). The American train pictured here is on a new railway in Peru. This increase in trade made vast fortunes for a few people, but most people in Latin America remained very poor.

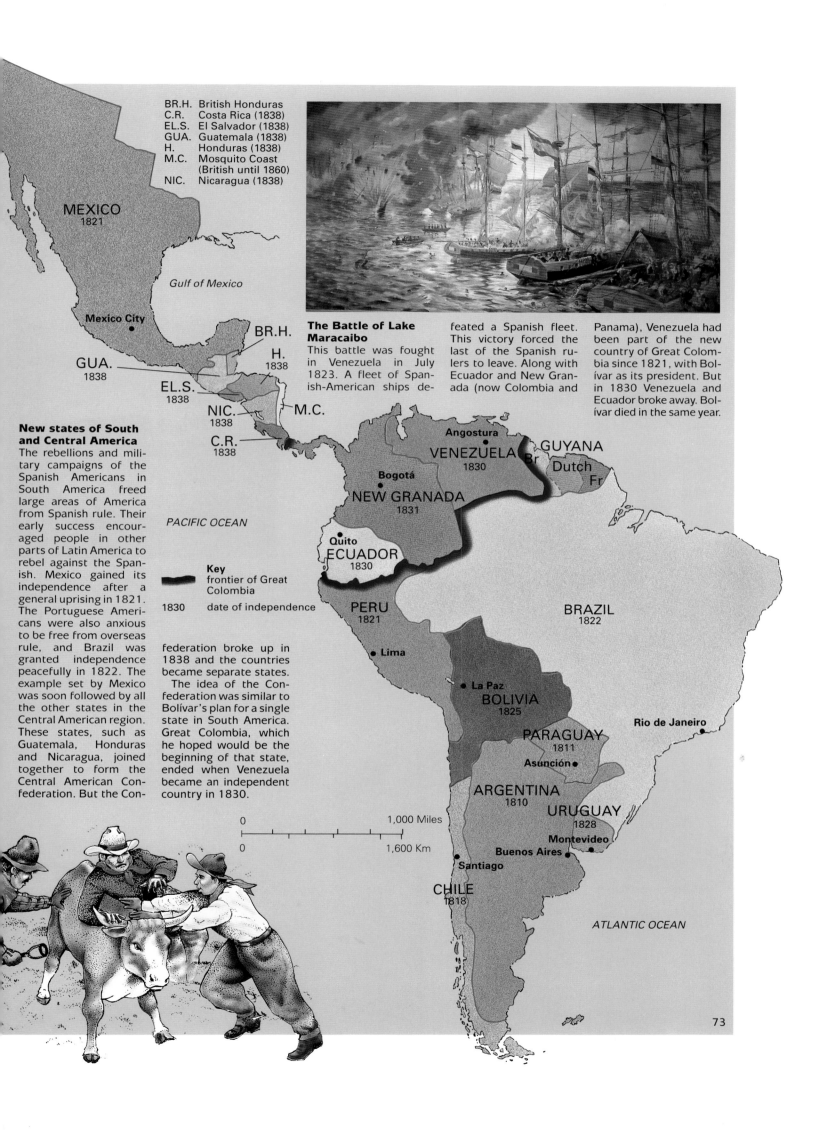

BR.H. British Honduras
C.R. Costa Rica (1838)
EL.S. El Salvador (1838)
GUA. Guatemala (1838)
H. Honduras (1838)
M.C. Mosquito Coast
(British until 1860)
NIC. Nicaragua (1838)

MEXICO
1821

Gulf of Mexico

Mexico City

BR.H.

GUA.
1838

H.
1838

EL.S.
1838

NIC.
1838

M.C.

C.R.
1838

The Battle of Lake Maracaibo

This battle was fought in Venezuela in July 1823. A fleet of Spanish-American ships de- feated a Spanish fleet. This victory forced the last of the Spanish ru- lers to leave. Along with Ecuador and New Gran- ada (now Colombia and Panama), Venezuela had been part of the new country of Great Colom- bia since 1821, with Bol- ívar as its president. But in 1830 Venezuela and Ecuador broke away. Bol- ívar died in the same year.

New states of South and Central America

The rebellions and mili- tary campaigns of the Spanish Americans in South America freed large areas of America from Spanish rule. Their early success encour- aged people in other parts of Latin America to rebel against the Span- ish. Mexico gained its independence after a general uprising in 1821. The Portuguese Ameri- cans were also anxious to be free from overseas rule, and Brazil was granted independence peacefully in 1822. The example set by Mexico was soon followed by all the other states in the Central American region. These states, such as Guatemala, Honduras and Nicaragua, joined together to form the Central American Con- federation. But the Con- federation broke up in 1838 and the countries became separate states.

The idea of the Con- federation was similar to Bolívar's plan for a single state in South America. Great Colombia, which he hoped would be the beginning of that state, ended when Venezuela became an independent country in 1830.

PACIFIC OCEAN

Key
━━━ frontier of Great Colombia

1830 date of independence

Angostura

VENEZUELA
1830

GUYANA
Br

Dutch

Fr

Bogotá

NEW GRANADA
1831

Quito
ECUADOR
1830

PERU
1821

Lima

BRAZIL
1822

La Paz

BOLIVIA
1825

PARAGUAY
1811

Asunción

Rio de Janeiro

ARGENTINA
1810

URUGUAY
1828

Montevideo

Buenos Aires

Santiago

CHILE
1818

ATLANTIC OCEAN

0 _____ 1,000 Miles

0 _____ 1,600 Km

THE EXPANSION OF THE UNITED STATES

NORTH AMERICA was originally settled by the British, French, Spanish and Dutch. The British captured New Amsterdam from the Dutch in 1664 and called it New York. By 1733 there were 13 British colonies on the east coast. In 1763 the British also gained control of French territories in the Mississippi valley.

The colonies grew angry because they had to pay taxes to Britain but had no representatives in the British parliament. In 1775 they began to fight the British and in 1776 declared their independence from Britain. The war, which lasted six years, was won by the Americans. In 1783 the United States of America was born. Each state had its own government, but they also needed a central, or Federal, government to make decisions about things which affected them all. They created a Constitution, or basic set of laws, and set up an elected parliament, or Congress, to make the laws for the new country.

Mississippi steamboat

The Mississippi River provided a way of transporting the produce of the southern states to new markets, but ships were needed which could cope with the strong current. The paddle-steamer was the answer. It could sail in shallow water and had a powerful steam engine which turned a large paddlewheel.

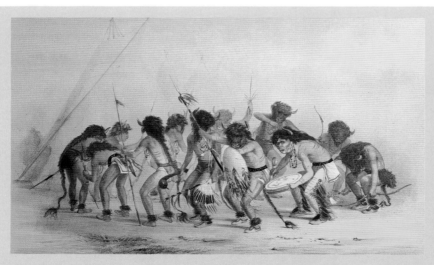

Indians of the Great Plains

The vast and fertile plains of the United States were occupied by Native Americans, or Indians as they were called. White settlers moved onto the plains during the 19th century. They took land from the Indians and shot the bison, which the Indians needed for food and clothing. The Indians fought hard for their lands but were defeated by the American troops. Eventually the Federal government made a treaty with the Indians, promising them land which would belong to them forever. Despite this, more settlers moved westward, the treaties were broken, and more land was taken from them. By 1890 all the remaining Indians were living on reservations. These are special areas set aside for them.

Looking for gold

The Americans captured California from the Mexicans in 1846–47. California is on the west coast of America, and its development began with gold. In 1848 a carpenter in California discovered gold nuggets in a stream. When the news reached the east coast of America in 1849, over 80,000 people traveled across America hoping to make their fortunes. This is known as the Californian Gold Rush. When they got to California they staked out stretches of water and, using pans, washed soil from the stream beds. Some did find gold and made their fortune, but most of them failed and lots of them died.

George Washington
George Washington (1732–99), commander in chief of the American army, led the Americans to victory in the war against the British. He helped draw up the American Constitution, and in 1789 became the first president of the United States of America.

Abraham Lincoln
Abraham Lincoln (1809–65) was president of the United States during the Civil War. He was assassinated in 1865 but the war had been won.

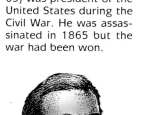

Union troops in the Civil War

The southern states of America grew cotton, tobacco, rice and sugar on large plantations. The workers on these plantations were black slaves, and slavery was essential to the prosperity of the south. The northern states were against slavery, and the southern states became afraid that the Federal government would abolish it throughout the United States. In 1860 seven southern states, led by South Carolina, left the United States of America, or the Union. They formed a new country of their own, called the Confederate States of America. In 1861 civil war broke out between the Confederate states and the Union states.

The Union troops were better equipped and had more food than the Confederate troops, and the northern states won the war. By the time the war ended in 1865, over 600,000 men from both sides had been killed.

The southern states were devastated by the war, but slavery was abolished in all the states. Over four million slaves were freed after the war, and the states of America were again united.

The expansion of the United States

In 1803 France sold its remaining territories to the Americans for 15 million dollars, and as a result the United States doubled in size. Texas joined the Union in 1845, the British handed over Oregon in 1846, and the Americans took California and New Mexico from the Mexicans in 1846–7. At this point American territory stretched from the Atlantic to the Pacific, but a lot of the land was still not settled. The development of the railroads in the 1860s made it much easier for Americans to move westward and settle the huge territories, which were now part of the Union. The Americans were joined by large numbers of immigrants, who came from Europe. Many of them had left their home countries because of famine or political persecution.

Key

	the original 13 colonies
	gained from Britain in 1783
	bought from France in 1803
	gained from Spain in 1810, 1812
	gained from Britain in 1818, 1842
	bought from Spain in 1819
	gained from Mexico in 1845
	gained from Britain in 1846
	gained from Mexico in 1848, 1853
——	northern boundary of the Confederate States

AL.	Alabama
CON.	Connecticut
DEL.	Delaware
IN.	Indiana
MASS.	Massachusetts
MD.	Maryland
MISS.	Mississippi
N.H.	New Hampshire
N.J.	New Jersey
PEN.	Pennsylvania
R.I.	Rhode Island
VT.	Vermont
W.V.	West Virginia

NATION STATES IN EUROPE

AT THE END OF the Napoleonic Wars, most of Europe was controlled by four major empires: French, Austrian, Russian and Turkish. In countries conquered by French armies, many people were angry. This anger, and the idea from the French Revolution that the people, not rulers, should control their country, spread throughout Europe and led to the development of nationalism. This is the idea that people with the same language and traditions should be in one state, which they themselves control. As a result, many new states were created in Europe during the 19th century, following rebellions, wars and political treaties. Among these states were Greece, Belgium, Italy and Germany. Industrial development was gathering speed at this time and many of Europe's nations became wealthy. They also extended their influence and the market for their goods abroad, by conquering and occupying countries throughout the world, making empires for themselves. This is known as imperialism.

A Bessemer Converter
In 1856 a British man, Henry Bessemer, invented a quick and cheap process for converting iron into steel. Steel is much stronger than iron and it was soon being used for ships, railways and many manufactured goods.

Paris in about 1875
The industrial revolutions in Europe drew many people from the countryside to towns and cities. In Paris the population grew from 500,000 in 1801 to almost 3 million in 1911.

Grand new buildings were built for these capital cities of empires, and transport and sewage systems were modernized. However, many people lived in poverty, in the cities' slums.

An early automobile
In 1885–86, Benz and Daimler developed the first motor vehicles with internal combustion engines, using gasoline as a fuel. Benz's vehicle had a top speed of 8 miles per hour.

Tea-pickers in Ceylon
The empires created by imperialism also provided Europe with cheap food, and raw materials for industry. In the 19th century Britain had the world's biggest empire, occupying about 6.75 million square miles of territory on every continent, and ruling over 400 million people. These tea-pickers worked on a British plantation in Ceylon (now Sri Lanka). The second-largest overseas empire was owned by France.

Europe in 1880

The move toward nationalism in the 19th century led to the creation of two new European states: the kingdom of Italy and the German Empire. By 1870 the states of Italy were united, due to the work of Giuseppe Garibaldi (1807–82) and Count Cavour (1810–61), the Prime Minister of Piedmont. Garibaldi's military campaigns helped to free southern Italy, and Cavour, with the help of France and Prussia, defeated the Austrians, who occupied much of northern Italy.

The Prime Minister of Prussia, Otto von Bismarck (1815–98), created a unified German state in 1871. He gained control of two states from Austria in 1866 and, by showing strength against France in the Franco-Prussian War, persuaded the southern German states to join the new German nation.

A Russian war with Turkey led to Greece, Serbia, Montenegro and Romania becoming independent of Turkish rule, and Belgium became independent of the Kingdom of the Netherlands.

Key
■ city with more than 1 million inhabitants
● city with 500,000 – 1 million inhabitants

1. BELGIUM
2. BOSNIA/HERZEGOVINA
3. LUXEMBOURG
4. MONTENEGRO
5. SERBIA
6. SWITZERLAND

THE DECLINE OF CHINA

WHILE EUROPEAN nations were developing into modern states, the Qing dynasty continued to rule China in its traditional way. It did not modernize China, and by the 19th century its rule was inefficient and corrupt. Most of the population lived in the country. These peasants were poor and heavily taxed. Europeans still traded with China but were not allowed to settle there. They had to pay for China's goods, such as porcelain, tea and silk, with gold or silver. But the British began to buy goods with opium (a drug), which was produced very cheaply in India. Chinese officials tried to ban this trade, and Britain went to war with China to force them to allow it. As a result of winning the first Opium War, Britain was given Hong Kong, and five Chinese ports were opened to foreign trade. These were called "treaty ports," and by the end of the century there were over 50. The Chinese people resented this European control and realized the Qing dynasty was weak. Several rebellions followed. Eventually the dynasty was overthrown, and in 1911 China was declared a republic.

The Chinese cake
Britain's success against China and the profits it made from its port of Hong Kong led other European countries to demand the same trading rights. Russia and Germany took control of other parts of China, and in 1894 Japan attacked China and seized Taiwan. This cartoon shows Britain, Germany, Russia, France and Japan dividing China between themselves. The European rulers of these areas treated the Chinese badly, using them as cheap labor and taxing them. This angered many Chinese and anti-European feeling was common.

East and West
As trade between China and Europe grew, China became increasingly influenced by European styles. The influence on Chinese life can be seen here. The girl sits on a typical English chair of the 1890s – but her dress is still Chinese and her feet are bound.

Hong Kong
British traders had for a long time been attracted to Hong Kong's splendid harbor. Britain gained Hong Kong after the Opium wars ended in 1860. Hong Kong became part of the British Empire and a major center of trade in Asia. In 1895 Britain gained more land near Hong Kong, on the mainland. They called this land The New Territories. It was secured on a 99-year lease from 1898.

The Boxer Rebellion

"Boxer" was a nickname given to members of a secret society called the "Righteous and Harmonious Fists." They were trained as soldiers and their aim was to drive foreigners out of China. In 1900 they began a revolt known as the Boxer Rebellion. They attacked Christians and foreign officials in Beijing and Tianjin. An army made up of soldiers from Europe, the United States and Japan crushed the rebellion and then looted parts of Beijing. This increased the hatred the Chinese felt for their rulers and the foreigners.

Key

- extent of the Qing Empire in 1800
- boundary between Inner and Outer China
- boundary between Inner and Outer Mongolia
- area of the Boxer Rebellion in 1900–1
- Great Wall of China
- ◉ treaty port opened by 1895

China in the 19th century

China's vast size had always made it difficult to govern. In the 19th century, secret societies defied the emperor's authority. They represented the many Chinese who hated the Qing dynasty for being northern "barbarians" who had given rights to foreign powers. After the Boxer Rebellion in 1900 many Chinese began to support the Guomindang party. Its aim was to overthrow the Chinese Empire and make China a modern, democratic state, free of foreign control. After several more rebellions the Qing dynasty ended in 1911, and China was made a republic in 1912.

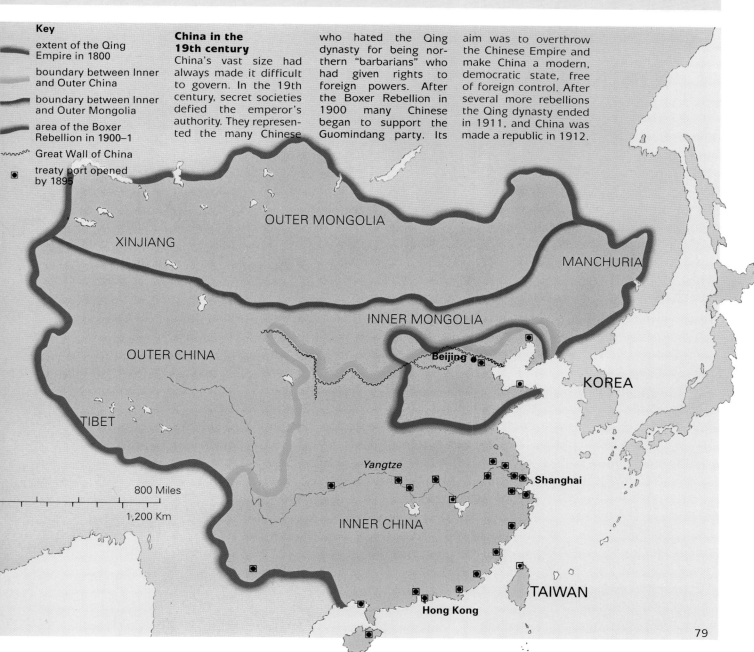

OUTER MONGOLIA

XINJIANG

MANCHURIA

INNER MONGOLIA

OUTER CHINA

Beijing

KOREA

TIBET

Yangtze

Shanghai

800 Miles

1,200 Km

INNER CHINA

TAIWAN

Hong Kong

THE TWENTIETH CENTURY

World wars, religious conflicts and tension between East and West, but great technological advances.

EUROPE

● 1914–18: almost all of Europe is involved in the First World War. France, Britain, Italy and the US defeat Germany and the Austro-Hungarian Empire.

● 1917: the Bolsheviks, or Communists, seize power in Russia and create the world's first communist state, later named the Soviet Union.
● The treaties which end the war lead to much bitterness in Germany and help Hitler and his National Socialist (Nazi) Party to power in 1933.
● In Italy a fascist dictator, Mussolini, is in power from 1922.

● 1939–45: the Second World War. In 1940 German troops occupy Paris (below).
● 1945: after Germany's defeat in the war a state of tension, the

Cold War, emerges between the Soviet Union and the West.
● 1957: six leading European nations form the European Economic Community (EEC).

MIDDLE EAST

● 1917: Britain's "Balfour Declaration" promises the Jewish people a homeland in Palestine.
● Turkey loses its Middle Eastern lands to Britain and France after

defeat in the First World War.
● 1923: Kemal Ataturk (below) becomes the first President of Turkey. He modernizes the country.

● 1948: Israel is proclaimed an independent Jewish state. War with neighboring Arabs begins.
● 1952: in Egypt army officers seize power from King Farouk.

● 1956: Egypt takes over the Suez Canal. Israel invades Egypt, and Britain and France move in to occupy the canal, but all are soon forced to withdraw.

AFRICA

● In South Africa Jan Smuts leads Union forces against German colonies in the First World War. He becomes Premier of South Africa in 1919.
● 1919: Germany surrenders all its African colonies after its defeat in the First World War.
● In Rhodesia, Britain hands power to a small minority of white settlers.
● 1922: Egypt declares itself independent, free of British rule.

● 1935: Italy invades Ethiopia, to add to its African empire of Libya, Italian Somaliland and Eritrea. The Ethiopian emperor, Haile Selassie, is exiled.

● 1940–43: British troops fight German and Italian forces in North Africa in the Second World War. German and Italian forces are driven into Tunisia

and surrender in May 1943.
● 1950s: many independence movements grow up among Europe's African colonies. Sometimes the Africans use violence to free themselves. The French are driven out of Algeria, 1958–62. In Kenya the Mau Mau conducts a campaign of violence against British rule, 1952–56.
● 1960: Nigeria wins independence from Britain.

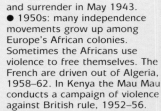

ASIA AND AUSTRALASIA

● Australian troops support Britain in the First World War.
● In India the Indian National Congress, the independence movement, is led by Mahatma Gandhi. It succeeds in focusing world attention on its campaign to free India from British rule.
● 1927: Australia moves its capital from Melbourne to Canberra.
● In China a long civil war is fought between the Communist

Peoples' Liberation Army led by Mao Zedong, and the Guomindang led by Chiang Kai-Shek. The civil war is halted while both sides fight Japan, 1937–45.

● 1939–45: Australia and New Zealand fight against Germany and Japan in the Second World War.
● 1945: Japan surrenders after the US drops atomic bombs on

Hiroshima (left) and Nagasaki.
● 1949: Chinese communists under Mao defeat the Guomindang.
● 1954: Vietnam divides into North and South.

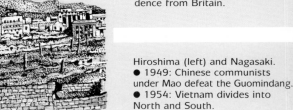

NORTH AND SOUTH AMERICA

● 1917: the United States enters the First World War on the side of the Allies, and helps achieve a victory over Germany and Austria-Hungary.
● 1929: on Wall Street, stock market shares drop sharply, helping to bring about the Great Depression.
● From 1930 Brazil is led by a dictator, Vargas, who introduces a form of fascism.

● In Mexico in the 1930s the government tries to improve the lives of the peasants and workers.
● 1928: Walt Disney (above) introduces Mickey Mouse.

● 1941: the United States is drawn into the Second World War when Japan attacks the US fleet at Pearl Harbor. The US plays a vital role in defeating both Japan and Germany.
● 1959: in Cuba Fidel Castro (right) leads an army of 800 men against the dictatorship of Batista. Batista is overthrown and Castro leads Cuba towards communism.

● 1962: the US and Soviet Union almost start a nuclear war over Soviet nuclear missiles on Cuba. The Soviets eventually agree to remove them.

The twentieth century experiences two devastating world wars. Both leave Germany defeated. Europe tries to heal the divisions of the past by creating the European Community.

Russia becomes the world's first communist state and communism spreads to China, Eastern Europe and southeast Asia. The Cold War, between the West and communist countries in Europe, leads both to produce many nuclear weapons. The "war" ends after 45 years of tension.

Africa and Asia are freed from colonial rule, and Japan becomes an economic superpower. In the Middle East there is constant tension between Palestinians and Israelis.

The century also brings remarkable scientific and technological advances.

● 1968: Soviet troops invade Czechoslovakia (below) to stop the attempts of the government, led by Dubcek, to create a democratic socialist system.

● 1967: the Six Day War between Israel and its Arab neighbors Egypt, Syria and Jordan.
● 1979: Egypt and Israel sign a peace agreement.

● 1964: Nelson Mandela is sentenced to life imprisonment for what the South African government calls "high treason."
● 1967: the South African surgeon Christiaan Barnard performs the world's first heart transplant operation. The patient lives for 18 days.
● 1969: the King of Libya is overthrown in a military coup led by Colonel Gaddafi.

● 1975: in Cambodia (later Kampuchea) a communist regime (the Khmer Rouge) comes to power, led by Pol Pot. It carries out mass murders (below).

● 1963: US President John F. Kennedy is assassinated in Texas.
● 1965: the first American combat troops arrive in Vietnam, sent to stop the spread of

● 1969: conflict breaks out in Northern Ireland between Catholics and Protestants. The Irish Republican Army (IRA) begins a terrorist campaign to force Britain out of Northern Ireland and create a united Ireland.
● 1975: the death in Spain of General Franco, dictator since 1939. Spain is led by its king, Juan Carlos, toward democracy.

● 1979: in Iran the Shah, or ruler, is deposed in a revolution which brings to power strong supporters of Islam, led by the Ayatollah Khomeini (below).

● 1970: Biafran civil war ends.
● 1971: in Uganda General Idi Amin takes over after a coup.
● 1975: Portugal declares all its African colonies independent.

● 1976: death of Mao Zedong in China. His successor, Deng Xiaoping, dismantles much of Mao's economic system.
● 1978: Pol Pot is overthrown.

communism from the north. The US is defeated in 1975.
● 1974: US President Richard Nixon resigns because of his involvement in the Watergate Scandal.

● 1982: Great Britain defeats Argentina in a brief war over who owns the Falkland Islands after Argentina occupies them in April.
● 1985: Mikhail Gorbachev becomes President of the Soviet Union. He is committed to economic reform.
● 1989: communism collapses in Eastern Europe. The Berlin Wall is pulled down by joyful Berliners.
● 1991–95: civil war leads to

● 1980: Iraq attacks Iran, beginning a war that will last eight years.
● 1990: Iraq invades Kuwait.
● 1991: after Iraq's invasion of Kuwait the US leads a United Nations force to drive the Iraqis out of the state.
● 1994: Israel withdraws from the Gaza Strip and Jericho area of the West Bank, leaving the Palestinians in control,

● 1980: Rhodesia is the last British colony in Africa to gain independence. It is now called Zimbabwe. Robert Mugabe is the first prime minister.
● 1990: Nelson Mandela of the African National Congress political party is freed after 27 years in prison.
● 1993: the South African laws of apartheid are dismantled. President Frederik de Klerk and

● 1984: Indira Gandhi, India's Prime Minister, is assassinated by two of her bodyguards.
● 1984: Britain signs an agreement to return Hong Kong

● 1981: the United States launches the Space Shuttle, the first crewed spacecraft that can be used more than once (above).

the breakup of Yugoslavia. War in Bosnia follows, between Serbs, Croats and Muslims. Many lives are lost, and buildings destroyed (below).

as was agreed in 1993.
● 1995: the Israeli leader, Yitzhak Rabin, is assassinated by an Israeli opposed to Rabin's concessions to the Palestinians.

Nelson Mandela are jointly awarded the Nobel Peace Prize.
● 1994: Mandela (below) takes over as South Africa's first black president.

to Chinese rule in 1997.
● 1989: a student protest for democracy in Beijing's Tiananmen Square is crushed by the Chinese army and many are killed.

● 1984: after the 1979 revolution, the left-wing Sandinistas, under Daniel Ortega, win the Nicaraguan election with 63 percent of the vote. Relations between the US and Soviet Union improve as the Cold War ends. Both sides destroy many nuclear weapons.
● 1993: Bill Clinton is inaugurated as the 42nd President of the United States.

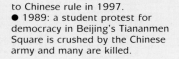

1963   1980   2000

THE FIRST WORLD WAR

FOLLOWING ITS creation as a single state, Germany became a military power. Many countries in Europe formed alliances to protect themselves against attack by the Germans. This in turn threatened Germany, and it began to build a large army and navy. Several other countries did the same. As the new and old nations jostled for power, war became more likely. One of the other new nations, Serbia, wanted to take Bosnia from Austria. When in 1914 the Austrian Archduke Ferdinand was assassinated by a Serbian revolutionary in Bosnia, the Austrians declared war on Serbia. Russia then declared war on Austria, and Germany declared war on Russia and France. When Germany invaded Belgium in order to attack the French army, Britain and Belgium declared war on Germany. The First World War had begun. The war was fought in two main areas: the Western Front in France and Belgium, and the Eastern Front in Poland and Russia.

Fighting in the trenches

The British and French armies stopped the German army 20 miles from Paris. Neither side could move forward, and so they dug trenches to protect themselves from the enemy. These trenches stretched from Belgium to Switzerland. Soldiers defended the trenches with machine guns which could fire 600 bullets a minute. Attacks against trenches defended by machine guns were a cause of huge numbers of deaths in the war. At least eight million soldiers were killed during four years of war.

Russian women in industry

Over 65 million men fought in the war and this meant that large numbers of women had to take over their jobs. In most countries it was the first time that women had worked in factories and on farms, and attitudes to women changed. Before the war the suffragette movement in Britain had been campaigning for women to have the right to vote. The work they did in the war helped them eventually to win this right.

US navy recruitment

The United States entered the war against Germany in April 1917. This was a big boost for the Allies. The US government issued recruitment posters. The poster below was made to encourage Americans to join the navy by appealing to their patriotism.

Lenin
Lenin was a Russian revolutionary communist. In 1917 the Russian tsar was overthrown. Later, Lenin's communist party, the *bolsheviks*, seized power. Lenin promised to feed the people and give them land. He made peace with Germany in 1918. Three years of civil war followed in Russia.

A British tank
Tanks are vehicles with thick armor, that carry guns. They were invented by the British during the First World War. They were very important in battle because they could move safely through the fire of machine guns and could also break through the enemy's line of trenches. However, tanks did have serious problems. They broke down easily and often became bogged down in the mud during battles. Bullets fired at tanks caused steel splinters to break away on the inside, badly cutting the crew.

Areas of fighting
In the First World War men fought not only in Europe, but also in Turkey, the Middle and Far East, and in European colonies worldwide. When Russia surrendered in March 1918, the Germans moved troops to the Western Front, hoping to break out of the trenches they had been fighting in for four years. But in 1917 America had declared war on Germany after its ships had been sunk by German submarines. British and French armies were joined by 1 million American soldiers. The Germans were forced to retreat. On the 11th hour of the 11th day of the 11th month of 1918 the Germans surrendered and were forced to accept a harsh peace treaty leading to economic ruin.

Key
- allies and their associates
- central powers
- neutral
- area affected by the Eastern Front
- area affected by the Western Front
- ✕ major battle

NORWAY
SWEDEN
DEN.
North Sea
GREAT BRITAIN
London
NETH.
BELG.
GERMANY
Berlin
POLAND
RUSSIA
Ypres
Somme
Paris
Verdun
Atlantic Ocean
FRANCE
SWITZ.
Vienna
AUSTRIA-HUNGARY
Caporetto
Tannenberg
PORTUGAL
Madrid
SPAIN
ITALY
CORSICA
Rome
SARDINIA
BOSNIA
SERBIA
MONT.
ALB.
ROMANIA
BULGARIA
Black Sea
OTTOMAN EMPIRE
Gallipoli
GREECE
TURKEY
SICILY
CRETE
Mediterranean Sea

0   500 Miles
0   800 Km

THE SECOND WORLD WAR

A FTER THE FIRST World War Germany had terrible economic problems. Attempts to solve them failed until Adolf Hitler became Germany's leader. He wanted to create an enlarged German nation containing all the German-speaking peoples of Europe. To achieve this he began to rebuild German military forces. This made the country strong again, and in 1938 and 1939 it occupied Austria and Czechoslovakia. In 1939 Hitler invaded Poland and, because of their promises to Poland, Britain and France declared war on Germany. By June 1940 Poland, Norway, Denmark, the Netherlands, Belgium and France had all been defeated by Germany. Also in 1940, Japan allied itself to Germany. Japan was the most powerful Asian country, and since the 1930s had been conquering its neighbors. This threatened the interests of the United States, Britain and the Soviet Union in the area. When in December 1941 Japan attacked the US navy base at Pearl Harbor in Hawaii, the US declared war on Japan and joined the global conflict.

The Nazis and the Jewish people of Europe

Hitler blamed the Jews for all Germany's problems. Hitler's successes at the beginning of the war meant that millions of Jews in Poland, Russia and other countries in Europe came under his control. Special squads of Nazis were formed to shoot any Jews they found. Millions of Jews were taken from their homes, as this picture shows, and transported to death camps. Six million Jews were murdered by the Nazis during the course of the war.

Fighting in Stalingrad

Germany and Russia had signed a treaty agreeing not to fight each other. When Germany invaded Russia in 1941, they were quickly able to conquer western Russia. Hitler wanted to occupy the whole of European Russia. But it is such a large country and the winters are so cold that the German advance soon slowed. In October 1942 the Germans attacked Stalingrad (now called Volgograd) and fought for control of the city for four months. In the end the Russians defeated the German army and forced it to surrender. Following this defeat the Russians gradually pushed the German armies back toward Germany.

The war in North Africa

After conquering most of Europe, Germany invaded North Africa to help Italy to defeat the British. They succeeded at first, but in November 1942 British and American troops landed in North Africa. By May 1943, after hard fighting, the Germans and Italians were driven out of North Africa.

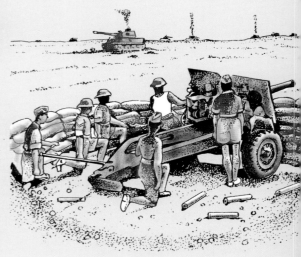

Adolf Hitler

After the First World War Adolf Hitler joined the National Socialist Workers' Party, or Nazi Party, and soon became its leader (*Führer*). In 1933 the Nazi Party won elections to the German parliament and Hitler became Chancellor of Germany.

Once Hitler came to power, he quickly moved to end all freedom in Germany. Newspapers other than those controlled by the Nazi party were closed down. By July 1933 all other political parties had been banned. The Nazi secret police, the Gestapo, hunted down opponents and imprisoned them. Many of the opponents died in jail. Hitler reduced unemployment in Germany by finding workers jobs in weapon factories. He planned to increase Germany's armed forces to create a Nazi empire in Europe. Hitler also gained popular support through large political spectacles, such as rallies at Nuremberg every year.

Hitler's empire

After declaring war on Germany, the British and French armies were cut off by the advancing Germans. The British army retreated to Dunkirk and was evacuated to England. Hitler planned to invade Britain, but the German air force, the *Luftwaffe*, was defeated by the Royal Air Force in the Battle of Britain. German airplanes then began to bomb British cities. Germany and its allies, known as the Axis powers, went on to occupy almost every country in Europe. Britain fought alone until 1941, when Germany invaded Russia and declared war on the USA. American troops assembled in Britain, and British and American airplanes began to bomb German cities.

With their vast numbers of men, ships, tanks and airplanes, together the Americans and Russians enabled the Alllies to defeat the Germans. In March 1945 American and Russian troops met in Germany. Hitler shot himself in April 1945 and in May the Germans surrendered to the Allies. The war in Europe was over, but the war in Asia continued until August.

The atomic bomb

In early 1945 US forces began to bomb Japanese cities, and they captured the island of Okinawa, only 500 miles south of Tokyo. Still Japan would not give up. In August 1945 the US decided to drop a secret weapon on Japan – the atomic bomb. On August 6, 1945, the first bomb destroyed the city of Hiroshima. Nagasaki was destroyed on August 9, and the Japanese surrendered. Atomic bombs make these huge mushroom-shaped clouds. The two bombs killed over 100,000 people but saved the lives of many Allied soldiers and ended the World War.

Key

area under Axis control in 1942

Allies

neutral countries

extent of Germany in 1937

extent of Germany in 1942

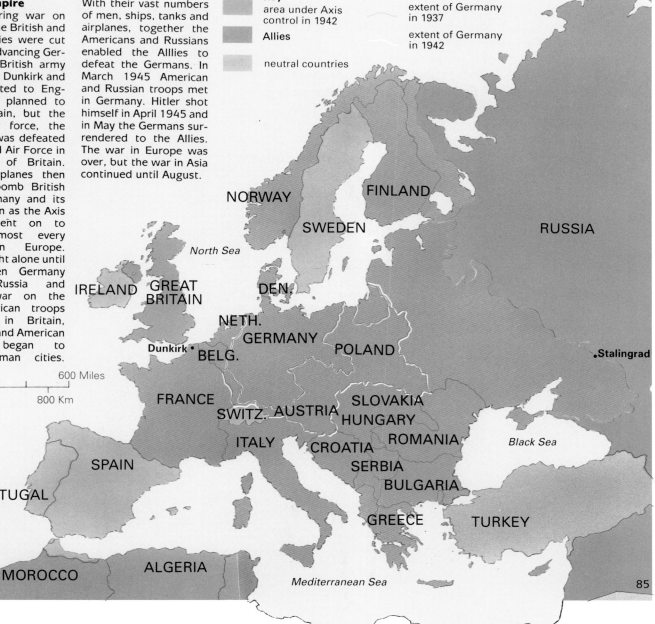

0   600 Miles

0   800 Km

NORWAY

FINLAND

SWEDEN

RUSSIA

North Sea

IRELAND

GREAT BRITAIN

DEN.

NETH.

GERMANY

POLAND

Dunkirk

BELG.

Stalingrad

FRANCE

SWITZ.

AUSTRIA

SLOVAKIA

HUNGARY

ITALY

CROATIA

ROMANIA

Black Sea

SPAIN

SERBIA

BULGARIA

PORTUGAL

GREECE

TURKEY

MOROCCO

ALGERIA

Mediterranean Sea

INDEPENDENCE IN ASIA AND AFRICA

A FTER THE RISE of the European nation states in the 19th century, the countries of Europe decided to occupy land in Africa. Some of them wanted to add to the empires they already had in Asia. North Africa was taken from the Ottoman empire, and most of the rest of the continent was taken from native Africans. This is called the "Scramble for Africa," and by 1914 there were only two independent countries in the continent, Ethiopia and Liberia. The Europeans intended to develop and rule their empires in Asia and Africa for hundreds of years, but more and more peoples began to demand the right to govern themselves. The colonial powers were too weakened by the Second World War to resist these calls for independence. Also, many Europeans no longer believed in empires, the United States of America was pressing them to make countries independent, and Russia (then the Soviet Union) was encouraging the independence movements. From 1946 onward Asian and African countries became independent. The age of the colonial powers was over.

India becomes independent

Britain ruled almost all of India from the early 19th century. In 1885 Indians founded the Indian National Congress to work for independence. In the 1920s and 1930s, Mahatma Gandhi and Jawaharlal Nehru led peaceful protests against British rule. India finally became independent in August 1947, soon after the Second World War. But there was religious hatred and rivalry in India. As a result two separate countries, India (Hindu) and Pakistan (Muslim), were formed.

In 1971 Pakistan itself split into two separate countries as East Pakistan broke away from West Pakistan after a civil war. East Pakistan became known as Bangladesh.

France's war in Algeria

France had large colonial territories across Africa, and invaded Algeria in 1890. From 1954 onward the native Algerians demanded independence, but there were 2 million French settlers in Algeria and the French saw it as part of France. The Algerian National Liberation Front led by Ben Bella fought the French, and in 1962 Algeria finally became an independent country.

Nelson Mandela

In 1990 Nelson Mandela, the leader of the African National Congress, was released after 27 years in prison. Mandela had struggled to end apartheid in South Africa which treated the black majority as inferior. In 1994 the first free elections took place and Mandela's ANC won. Mandela became President.

Jawaharlal Nehru, 1889–1964

Jawaharlal Nehru became committed to independence for India when he returned home to India after being educated in England. In 1947 he became the first prime minister of independent India and worked hard to turn India into an industrial economy.

Independence since 1945

The first countries to become independent at the end of the Second World War were in Asia. Many had seen the colonial powers defeated by the Japanese and realized that they could fight for independence themselves. The communist state in China, created by Mao Zedong supported many communist independence movements in Asia. The Dutch

Jomo Kenyatta, c.1891–1978

Following the Mau Mau rebellion against the British, Kenya became independent in 1963. Jomo Kenyatta was Kenya's first prime minister. He encouraged white farmers and administrators to stay in Kenya after independence, to help the country to develop.

East Indies became the independent state of Indonesia after a nationalist uprising; the French were forced to leave Indochina; and the Americans granted independence to the Philippines.

Most of Asia was independent by 1957, and most of Africa by 1970. Many of these independent countries became economically dependent on the two superpowers, America and the Soviet Union (Russia).

The Middle East

After the Second World War, the Jews campaigned for their own state and were supported by the United Nations. In 1948 they set up their own state, called Israel, in a part of Palestine. Many Palestinian Arabs were forced out of their homes. This led to much fighting as the Israelis fought the Palestinians and nearby Arab states. Three wars followed in 1956, 1967 and 1973.

In 1993, however, the Israeli leader, Yitzhak Rabin, and the Palestinian leader, Yassir Arafat, signed a peace agreement (above). The Israelis agreed to hand back some land to the Palestinians in exchange for peace. However, in 1995 an Israeli assassinated Rabin. He said that the killing was a protest against the peace process with the Palestinians.

Key

colonial power before independence:

- Belgian
- British
- French
- German
- Italian
- Portuguese
- Spanish
- independent states in 1945

1956 date of independence

B.F.	Burkina Faso
CA	Cameroon
C.A.R.	Central African Republic
CO	Congo
E.G.	Equatorial Guinea
ER	Eritrea
GA	Gabon
U.A.E.	United Arab Emirates
UG	Uganda
ZI	Zimbabwe

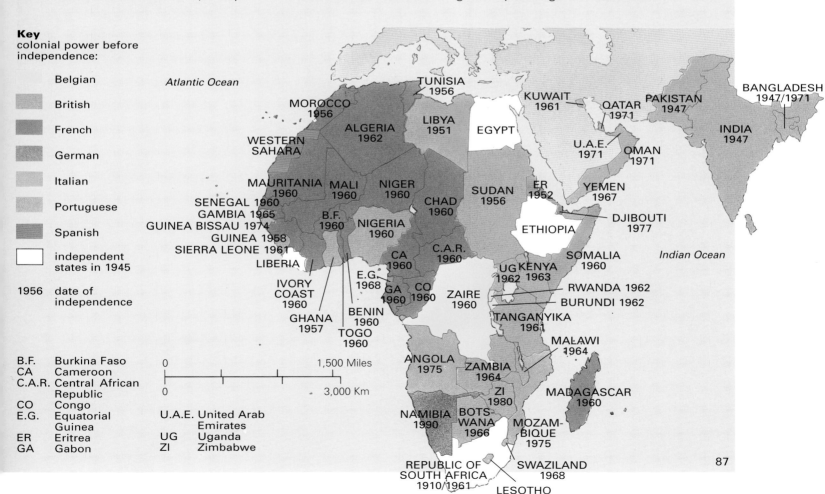

87

TOWARD A
NEW CENTURY

AFTER THE SECOND World War the two most powerful countries in the world were the United States of America and the Soviet Union. By 1949 the armies of these two "superpowers" were confronting each other across the borders of Eastern and Western Europe. In the 1950s and 60s the conflict between them became known as the "Cold War." Both the superpowers developed many nuclear bombs, more powerful even than those dropped on Japan, and the fear of a nuclear war was always present. The Cold War lasted until the beginning of the 1990s, when communist rule collapsed in Eastern Europe and the Soviet Union. Many countries became independent from the Soviet Union, and established themselves as nation states. The ending of the Cold War meant that the United States and Russia (formerly the Soviet Union) could now work together inside and outside the United Nations to try to solve international problems.

Mao Zedong
China is now the only major country in the world with a communist government. It was set up in 1949 when Mao Zedong (above) defeated the nationalist government after a long civil war. He worked hard to make China a prosperous country, with modern industries.

Genetic engineering
The 20th century has seen many advances in science. Genetic engineering is a process by which genes, made of DNA (right), can be changed. It could be used in the fight against various diseases.

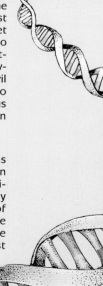

European Union
Europe was in ruins after the Second World War, but recovery soon began and by 1952 industrial production was 35 percent higher than before the war. West Germany became the strongest European industrial power. In 1957 Germany, France, Italy, Belgium, the Netherlands and Luxembourg formed the European Economic Community (EEC), agreeing to abolish trade taxes between themselves and to impose them on imports from other countries. The EEC expanded as more nations, such as Britain, Spain and Ireland, joined. The parliament of the EEC (now renamed the European Union) meets at Strasbourg in France.

88

The fall of communism

After the Second World War the Soviet Union set up communist governments in Poland, East Germany, Czechoslovakia, Romania and Bulgaria. These countries were firmly controlled by the Soviets. In 1989 and 1990 the people of these countries rose up against their communist rulers. Gorbachev did not use troops to crush the protesters, and so the countries of Eastern Europe were able to set up their own democratic, non-communist governments. The end of communism in East Germany was symbolized by the bringing down of the Berlin Wall in 1989 (left).

Mikhail Gorbachev

Gorbachev became the Soviet leader in 1985. He wanted to make it a freer and more wealthy, but still communist, country. He resigned in 1991 when communism was overthrown and the Soviet Union began to break up into independent countries.

A global challenge

Damage to the environment continues to be one of the greatest problems facing the world today. In 1992, at an "Earth Summit" in Brazil, the world's leaders signed a pledge to protect "biodiversity" – the total variety of life on Earth. But there is still much to be done.

Desertification is the creation of deserts by changes in climate, overgrazing and the cutting down of trees. It can be controlled by planting special grasses and trees to stop the soil from blowing away.

Forests are also being destroyed by the effects of acid rain, which is caused by burning fuels like coal and oil, and pollution from car exhausts. Acid rain has particularly affected forests in Scandinavia, eastern Europe and eastern North America. Acid rain also kills fish in lakes and rivers. Oil pollution can also have terrible effects on the environment. Most oil spills occur when tankers run aground. In 1989 the *Exxon Valdez* ran aground off the shore of Alaska in America's worst oil disaster. The spilled oil killed 36,000 birds and 3,000 sea otters. Oil pollution was caused deliberately by the Iraqis during the Gulf War in 1991. Huge quantities of oil were released into the shallow waters of the Persian Gulf and oil fields were set alight.

International efforts have been made to reduce pollution, but many countries have done little to solve the problem. Alternatives need to be found to replace fossil-based fuels such as coal, oil and gas. Attempts are being made to use cleaner forms of energy, such as wind power.

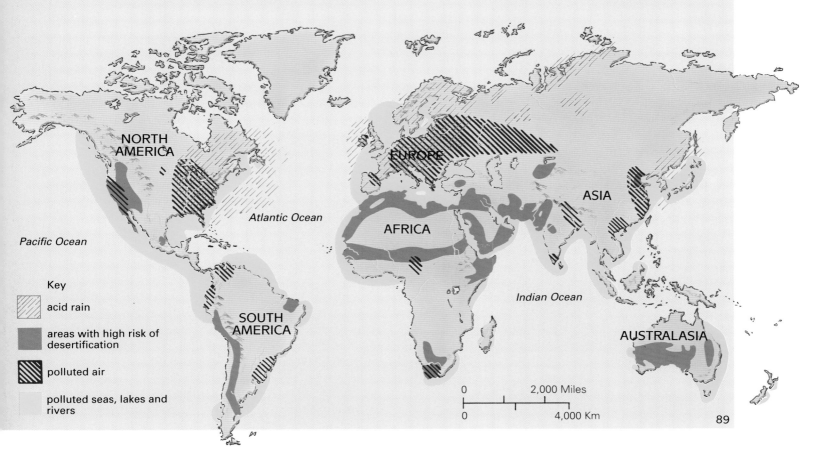

NORTH AMERICA

EUROPE

ASIA

Atlantic Ocean

AFRICA

Pacific Ocean

Indian Ocean

SOUTH AMERICA

AUSTRALASIA

Key

acid rain

areas with high risk of desertification

polluted air

polluted seas, lakes and rivers

0   2,000 Miles

0   4,000 Km

GLOSSARY

Agriculture   The growing of crops and the raising of animals for people's use.

Ally   A country that has a friendly agreement with one or more other countries.

Anatomy   The study of the body.

Aqueduct   A bridge, usually built on arches, built to carry flowing water.

Architect   A designer of buildings.

Aristocracy   A group of privileged and wealthy people; the nobility.

Astronomy   The study of the stars and planets and their movements.

Barbarian   Derived from the Latin word for "foreigner"; used to describe those who lived outside the Roman Empire.

Bolshevik   A member of the Communist Party that seized power in the Russian Revolution.

Bourgeoisie   The middle class of people, such as teachers, lawyers, doctors and owners of businesses.

Bronze   An alloy (mixture) of copper and tin.

Buddhism   A religion that began in India, which teaches that the main cause of suffering is people's desire for pleasure, and that the way to real peace is to overcome this desire.

Caliph   A successor to Muhammad as spiritual ruler of the Islamic Empire.

Capitalism   An economic system in which trade and industry are controlled by private owners, and goods are bought and sold in a free market.

Charcoal   A black material used for fuel, made by burning wood slowly in an oven.

Christianity   A religion that teaches that Jesus of Nazareth was Christ, the Son of God.

Citizen   An inhabitant of a city; a person with full legal rights in a country.

City-state   A city that rules itself and the land around it.

Civilization   A settled way of life, which involves people living in towns or cities.

Civil war   A war fought between different groups of people within the same country.

Cold war   A state of conflict between countries, involving no actual fighting.

Colony   A group of people living in an area or country under the rule of another country.

Communism   An economic and political system in which industry is owned by the state and not private individuals.

Constitution   A set of laws by which a country is ruled and in which the powers of the government are set out.

Culture   The values and way of life of a people; includes the arts, such as music, literature, painting and sculpture.

Cyrillic alphabet   The alphabet invented in the 9th century by a priest, Cyril, for the Slavic languages of the Balkan peoples.

Democracy   A system of government in which the people of a state rule themselves either directly or through rulers they elect.

Dictatorship   A system of government in which the ruler holds complete power.

Domestication   The keeping of animals near people and their homes as a source of labor, food and clothing.

Economy   The way a country's resources are organized to produce wealth.

Empire   A number of countries or peoples under the rule of a single power.

Export   To send goods abroad for sale.

Fascism   A political system in which all power is held by a strong centralized state led by a dictator.

Federal government   A system of government in which some power is given to individual states within a country and some is kept by the central authority.

Hieroglyphics   Forms of writing that use picture-symbols to represent sounds and objects.

Hinduism   A religion that began in India. It teaches that Brahman is the supreme spirit. Its followers worship several different gods that are different aspects of Brahman.

Hoplite   A heavily armed and well-trained Greek foot soldier.

Imperialism   The extending of power of a nation over other, weaker countries.

Import   To bring goods into a country from other countries or regions, for sale.

Independence   Self-rule for a colony, country or region; an end to its control by another country.

Islam   The religion preached by the Prophet Muhammad, whose followers must accept Allah as the one true God. It was founded in the early 7th century AD.

Janissary   A professional foot soldier of the Ottoman Empire.

Jew   A follower of the religion of Judaism.

Judaism   The religion of the Jews, based on the Hebrew Bible, the Torah.

Khanate   An area of the Mongol Empire ruled by the descendants of Genghis Khan.

Kiln   An oven used for hardening or drying such objects as pottery, tiles and bricks.

Latin   The language of the ancient Romans.

Locomotive   A railway engine. The first steam locomotive was built in 1804.

Martyr   A person who is killed for his or her ideals – often religious beliefs.

Mecca   The holy city of Islam.

Megalith   A huge stone placed in burial and ceremonial monuments, especially between 3200 and 1500 BC.

Mesoamerica   The area that is now Mexico and northern Central America.

Middle Ages   The period of history from c. AD 500 to 1500; the medieval period.

Missionary   A person who works to convert people to his or her religion, often traveling to other countries.

Monarchy   A system of government with a king or queen as ruler.

Mosaic   A picture made up of small pieces of colored material cemented together.

Mosque   A Muslim place of worship.

Muslim   A follower of the religion of Islam.

Nationalism   The idea that people with the same language and culture should rule themselves and not be governed by foreigners.

Nomad   A person who lives an unsettled life, usually wandering in search of food or grazing land for domesticated animals.

Oracle   A way in which the gods were thought to speak about the future or to give advice, especially in ancient Greece.

Patriarch   Founder or head, usually of certain religious groups; one of the five leaders of the early Christian Church.

Patron   A wealthy person who supports artists and writers in their work.

Pharaoh   A ruler of ancient Egypt.

Pictogram   A simple drawing used in an early form of writing to represent an object.

Philosophy   The study of knowledge and wisdom.

Pope   The head of the Christian Church until the Reformation and, since then, the head of the Roman Catholic Church.

Prehistory   The time before the invention of writing.

Protestant   A Christian who does not accept the authority of the Pope and the Roman Catholic Church.

Pyramid   A large stone structure with a base and four sloping or stepped sides, built by the Egyptians as royal tombs and by the Mayas and Aztecs as platforms for temples.

Quran   (also Koran) The holy book of Islam, which sets out how Muslims should live.

Raw material   A substance that occurs naturally in the world, and is processed, as in industry, to make other goods.

Reformation   The process of religious change in the 16th century in Europe, which led to a split in the Christian Church between Protestants and Roman Catholics.

Renaissance   The rebirth of interest in the cultures of ancient Greece and Rome, in Europe from the 14th through the 16th century.

Republic   A country that is not ruled by a king or queen.

Reservation   Land set aside by the government of the United States for the native peoples of North America.

Revolution   A complete and often violent change in the way a country is run (the French Revolution) or in its social and economic conditions (the Industrial Revolution).

Roman Catholic   A Christian who recognizes the Pope as the leader of the Church.

Satrapy   A province of the Persian Empire, ruled by a satrap.

Shogun   A military ruler in Japan.

Smelting   The process by which metal is removed from rock or mineral ore by heating it in a furnace.

Socialism   A political and economic system based on the idea that the people as a whole, or their government, should own and control the country's wealth.

Stupa   A mound built on top of Buddhist temples to contain holy relics.

Sufi   An Islamic holy man and teacher.

Superpower   A very powerful country that has great influence throughout the world.

Technology   The use of tools, science and inventions for supplying what people need to survive and be comfortable.

Temple   A place of religious worship, such as a church or synagogue.

Terracotta   A brownish-red unglazed pottery, made by baking clay.

Third World   The poorest countries of the world, in Asia, Africa and Latin America.

Treaty   A written agreement or alliance between two or more countries.

Tribute   A form of tax, paid by one ruler or country to another.

Tsar   (also Czar and Csar) The Russian term for emperor.

Viceroy   A person who governs as a representative of the ruler.

Ziggurat   A pyramid-shaped religious tower built in ancient Mesopotamia.

INDEX

Page numbers in *italics* refer to text with illustrations; numbers in **bold** refer to maps. Cross-references (*see* and *see also*) point you to another entry in the index.

A

Aachen *34*, **35**
Abbas I, emperor 50
Abbasid Empire/ dynasty 26, 32
Abdul Hamid II, Emperor 67
Abyssinia (*now* Ethiopia) *27*, *46*, **47**, *67*, 80, **87**
acid rain 89
Acre 27
Acropolis (Athens) 11
Afghanistan 23, **41**, 59
Africa 6, 10
   colonization **52-3**, 66-7
   kingdoms 27, 46-7, **47**
Afrikaners 66-7
afterlife 14, *15*, 17, *18*, 28, *36*
Agade **13**
agriculture 7, 8, **9**, 38, 90
   animals *8*, 10, *45*, *47*
   crops 9, 10, 16, 22, 75
   irrigation 10, *14*
   plowing *8*, *11*
Ajanta **41**
Akaba, king of Dahomey 50
Akbar the Great 50
Alabama **75**
Alaric the Goth 34
Alaska 57, 66, 89
Albania **83**
Alexander the Great 11, 20, **23**
Alexander II, Tsar 57, 67
Alexander III, Tsar 67
Alexandria *15*, **29**, **31**, *47*, **59**
Alfred, king of Wessex 37
Algeria 80, **85**, *86*, **87**
America *see* Mesoamerica; North America; South America
Amin, Idi 81
Amri *17*
Amsterdam *54*, **55**, *71*, *77*
   New Amsterdam *51*, 74
Amun (Egyptian priests) 11
Anasazi culture 27
Anatolia **21**, 58, **59**
anatomy *54*, 90
Ancient Egypt *see* Egypt
Ancient Greece *see* Greece
ancient history 12-25
   time-chart 11
Ancient Rome *see*

Roman Empire
Angevin Empire 27
Angkor Wat *27*, **41**
Anglo-Saxons 35
Angola 50, **87**
Angostura **73**
animals *8*, *25*, *26*, *45*, *47*
Antioch **25**, **29**, **31**
aqueduct *24*, 90
Arabia **59**
Arabs 26, 31, 32, 46, **47**, 80-1, 87
Arafat, Yassir *87*
Aragon, kingdom **39**
Argentina 72, **73**, 81
Aristotle 11, 23
Arizona **75**
Arkansas **75**
Arles 32
armies
   ancient *13*, *19*, 22
   medieval *31*, 37, 44, *45*, *58*
   weapons and armor *22*, *31*, 44, 45, 49, *51*, *62*
   modern *82–5*
Aryan kingdoms 11, 17
Asante (Ashanti) 51
Ashanti (Asante) 51
Ashoka (Asoka), king of Magadha 11, **17**, 40
Ashur **13**
Ashurbanipal, king of Assyria *11*, **13**
Asia, early history 6, **7**, **9**, 10-11
Asia Minor **23**
Asoka (Ashoka), king of Magadha 11, **17**, 40
Assyrian Empire *11*, **13**
astronomy 50, 54, 90
Asuka **41**
Asunción **73**
Ataturk, Kemal *80*
Athens 11, 22, **23**, **25**, **29**, **31**, 55
   Acropolis 11, *22*
atomic bombs 80, 81, 85, 88
Augustus, Roman emperor 11, *25*
Australia 6, 10, **65**, 80
Australopithecus 6
Austria 11, 51, 84, **85**
   Empire (Austria-Hungary) 66, 67, **71**, *77*, 80, 82, **83**
automobiles 76
Avanti *17*
Axum 26
Ayutthaya **41**
Ayyubid Empire/dynasty 27
Azerbaijan 58, **59**
Aztec Empire 27, 48, **49**, 50, **52**, *53*

B

Babur, Mughal emperor 58, **59**
Babylon 11, **13**, **21**
Bactria 21, **21**
Baghdad 32, **33**, 44, **45**, 58

Bahama Islands 52, **52**
Balfour Declaration 80
Balkans 31
Baltic Sea 27, **37**, **56**
Bangladesh 86, **87**
baobab tree *51*
barbarians 34-5, **35**, 90
Barnard, Christiaan 81
baths and toilets *24*
Batista, Fulgencio 80
Beijing (Peking) *61*, **61**, **79**
   Tiananmen Square 81
Belgium 67, 76, **77**, 88
   World Wars 82, **83**, 84, **85**
Ben Bella, Ahmed 86
Bengal 64
Benin 27, *46*, **47**, *51*, **87**
Benz, Karl 76
Berlin **39**, **55**, 77, **83**, **85**
   Wall 81, *89*
Bessemer, Henry 76
Bethlehem **29**
Biafra 81
Bible *28*, 29
Birmingham 69
Bismarck, Otto von 77
Black Death 27, *39*
Black Sea **37**
Blériot, Louis 67
Bogotá 72, **73**
Bolívar, Simón 72, 73
Bolivia 72, **73**
bolsheviks 83, 90
Bombay 51, **64**
Bonaparte, Napoleon 66, *70*, *71*, **71**
Borneo **65**
Borobudur **41**
Bosnia/Hercegovina **77**, 81, 82, **83**
Botany Bay **65**
Botswana **87**
Boxer Rebellion 67, *79*
Bradford **69**
Brazil 50, **52**, 80
   "Earth Summit" 89
bridges *24*, 49
Bristol **69**
Britain **55**, **77**, 88
   see also England; Scotland; Wales
   colonies 50-1, **64**, **65**, 74, **75**, *77*, *78*
   Industrial Revolution *68-9*, **69**
   Roman and medieval **25**, **35**, **37**
   trade **64**, 69
   wars *51*, **71**, 80, 82-5, 83, **85**
British Honduras **73**
bronze *see* metal-working
Bronze Age *8*, 10-11
Budapest **39**, **59**
Buddhism 11, 17, 26, 40-1, **41**, 90
   the Buddha *17*, 40
   temples *11*, *26*, 40, 41, *41*, *42*
Buenos Aires **73**
Buhen **15**

buildings *see* churches; fortresses; houses; temples
Bulgaria 10, **77**, **83**, **85**, 89
   Bulgars 31
Burgundians 35
burial *see* afterlife; graves and tombs
Burkina Faso **87**
Burma (*now* Myanmar) **41**, **61**
Burundi **87**
Byzantine Empire 25, 26, 30-1, **31**, **37**
   Byzantium (*later* Constantinople) **25**, 27, **30**, **31**

C

Cairo **15**, *33*, **47**
Calais 27
Calcutta 51, **64**
California 74, **75**
caliphs 32, 90
Calvin, John 54
Cambodia (*now* Kampuchea) 27, **41**, 81
Cameroon **87**
Canada, colonization 66
canals 21, *43*, **43**, **69**
Canberra 80
Cape Colony 66
   see also South Africa
   Cape of Good Hope 51
   Cape Town 51
Caporetto, battle **83**
Cardiff **69**
Carlisle **69**
Carnac 10
Carolingian Empire/ dynasty **34**, 35
Carrhae, battle 11
Carthage 11, *24*, **25**, **29**, **31**, 32
caste system 11, 17
Castile, kingdom 38, **39**
castles 27, 38, 39, *62*, *63*
Castro, Fidel 80
cataracts *15*
cave paintings 7
Cavour, Camillo 77
Celsius, Anders 51
Celtic cultures, Germany 11
Central African Republic **87**
Central America *see* Mesoamerica
Central American Confederation 73
Ceylon (*now* Sri Lanka) 26, 40, **41**, **64**, 77
Chad **87**
Chagatai Khanate 44, **45**
Champlain, Samuel de 50
Chanhu-Daro *17*
Charlemagne, Holy Roman emperor 26, 34, *35*, **35**
Charles I, king of England 50-1

Charles V, Holy Roman emperor 50
Charles X, king of France 66
Chavin culture 11
Cheng-chou **19**
Cherokee Indians 66
Chiang Kai-Shek 80
Chicago **75**
Chichén Itzá 26, *48*, **49**
child labor *68*
Chile 72, **73**
China
   ancient 9, 10, 11
   early period 18-19, **19**, 26, **41**
   Great Wall **19**, 42, 60
   medieval 27, 42-3, **43**, 44, 45
   Ming period 60, *61*
   Qing (Manchu) period 51, 60, **61**, 66-7, 78, **79**
   science and technology 42
   Taiwan (Formosa) **61**, 67, 78, **79**
   trade 52, 61, 63, 66
   twentieth century 67, 80-1, 87, *88*
china (porcelain) *61*
Chinghiz (Genghis) Khan 44, 45, **45**, 59
Christianity 26, 28-9, 30, 38, 90
   Catholics and Protestants 50, 51, 54
   spread of 26, **29**, *30*, 50, **60**, 62
churches 27, 28, 29, 30, *34*, *38*
cities and towns 38, 43, *54*, 76, **77**
   China and Japan 42, *43*, *62*
   city-states 12, 22, **47**, 90
   early 10, *11*, 12, 16-17, **17**, 26-7
   planned 16, *25*, 38
civil wars *75*, 83
Cleopatra, queen of Egypt 11
cloth weaving 10, *48*, 51
Clovis, king of the Franks 34
coal and coke *68*, **69**, 89
Cold War 80-1, 88, 90
Cologne **39**
Colombia **73**
colonies 50-1, 66-7, *77*, **83**, 86, 90
   Africa 50-1, **53**, *78*, 80, 86
   Americas **52-3**, 72, **73**, 74, 75
   Asia/Australasia **53**, 57, *64*, **64-5**, *78*
   independence 80-1, 86-7, **87**
Colorado **75**
Columbus, Christopher 52, **52-3**

92

communism 80-1, 81, 88, *89*, 90
Confederate States of America 75
Confederation of the Rhine 71
Confucius 11, 60
Congo (Belgian, *now* Zaire) 67, 87
Congo (French) 87
Connecticut 75
Constantine I, Roman emperor 29
Constantine XI, Byzantine emperor 31
Constantinople (*now* Istanbul) 29, *30*, **31**, *32*, **39**, 52, 55
   see also Byzantine Empire, Byzantium
Cook, James *65*, **65**
Copán 26
Copenhagen 55
Copernicus, Nicolaus 50
copper *see* metal-working
Cordoba 30
Corsica 25, 29, 31, **55**, **71**, **77**
Cortes, Hernán 50, *53*
Cossacks 51
Costa Rica 73
Crete 10, 23, 29, 31, 55
Croatia 85
Cromwell, Oliver 51
crusades 27
csar (tsar, czar) 91
Cuba 67, 80
Cuzco 27, *49*
Cyclades 10
Cyprus 25, 29, 31, 55
Cyrus the Great, king of Persia 20, 21
czar (csar, tsar) 91
Czechoslovakia 81, 84, 89
   Slovakia 85

D
Dahomey, kingdom 50
Daimler, Gottfried 76
Dakotas 75
Dakshinapatha **17**
Damascus 13, 29, 31, *32*, 33, **59**
Darby, Abraham 69
Darius I, king of Persia 20, **21**, 23
Darius III, king of Persia 11
Darlington **69**
David, king of Israel 11
death *see* afterlife; graves and tombs
Delaware **75**
Delhi **59**, **64**
Delphi *23*, **23**
democracy 90
Deng Xiaoping 81
Denmark and Danes **39**, **55**, **71**, **77**, **83**, 84, **85**
   Vikings 36, **37**
Depression, Great 80
Derby **69**
desertification **89**

Dias, Bartholomew 52
disease 27, *39*, 42, 53, 66
Disney, Walt *80*
Djibouti 87
Djoser, king of Egypt 10
Dnieper River **56**
domestication *8*, 10, 90
Dominican Republic 67
Dover **69**
Dubcek, Alexander 81
Dunkirk **85**
Dutch Republic *see* Netherlands
dynasty 42

E
Early Modern period 52-65
   time-chart 50-1
"Earth Summit" 89
East India companies 64, 67
East Indies (*now* Indonesia) 51, **65**, 87
   Moluccas (Spice Is) 50, 64, **65**
Easter Island 7
Eboracum (*now* York) **25**
Ecuador 72, **73**
Edinburgh **69**
Edo (*now* Tokyo) **63**
Egypt 59, 80-1, **87**
   Ancient 10-11, **13**, 14, *15*, **15**, 23, **25**
   foreign rule over 11, **13**, 21, 23, 66
   Muslim state 26-7
   St. Catherine's monastery *28*
El Salvador **73**
Elba **71**
Elizabeth, Tsarina 56
engineering *see* technology
England
   see also Britain
   Civil War 50-1, 54
   colonies 50-1
   industry **69**
   medieval 27, 37, 38, **39**
   Tudor and Stuart 50-1
Equatorial Guinea 87
Eridu 10
Eritrea 80, **87**
Essen *68*
Ethiopia (Abyssinia) 27, *46*, **47**, *67*, 80, **87**
Etruscan civilization 11
Euphrates Valley 11, **13**
Europe, ancient 6, *7*, *8*, *9*, 10
European Union (EEC, EU) *88*
exploration **52-3**, **64-5**, 66-7
Ezana, king of Axum 26

F
Fahrenheit, D.G. 51
Falkland Islands war 81
farming *see* agriculture
Farouk, king of Egypt 80
Fatehpur Sikri *50*

Feng **19**
Ferdinand, king of Spain 52
Ferdinand, Archduke 82
Fiji **7**, 65
Finland **39**, **56**, 85
First World War 82-3, **83**
flooding *14*, *18*
Florence 38, **39**, 55
Florida 75
Forbidden City (Beijing) *61*
forests 9, 38, 89
Formosa (Taiwan) **61**, 67, 78, **79**
fortresses 11, 16
   castles 27, 38, 39, *62*, *63*
France 51, **55**, 64, 66-7, **77**, 80, 88
   colonies 51, **64-5**, 74-5, *77*, *78*, 80, *86*
   early history 7, 9, *25*
   Gauls 11, 34
   medieval 35, 37, 38, **39**
   Napoleonic period 70–1
   Revolution 66, *70*
   World Wars 82-5, **83**, 84, 85
Francia and Franks 34, **35**
Franco, Francisco 81
Fulani people 66
Funj **47**

G
Gabon 87
Gaddafi, Muammar 81
Gallipoli 27
   battle **83**
Gama, Vasco da 50, **52**, **53**
Gambia 87
Gandhi, Indira 81
Gandhi, Mahatma 80, 86
Garibaldi, Guiseppe 77
gauchos *72-3*
Gaul (France) and Gauls 11, 34
Gautama Siddhartha (Buddha) 11, *17*, 40
Gaza Strip 81
Genghis (Chinghiz) Khan 44, *45*, **45**, 59
Genoa 55
Georgia (USA) **75**
Germany 11, 55, 67, 76, **77**, 88
   colonies *78*, 80
   Confederation of the Rhine **71**
   East Germany 89
   Holy Roman Empire 26, **39**, 51, **55**
   Industrial Revolution *68*, 76
   medieval **35**, 37, 38, **39**
   World Wars 80, 82-5, **83**, 85
Ghana (Gold Coast) 51, 67, **87**
Giza *14*, **15**
Glasgow **69**
glossary 90-1

Gloucester **69**
gods and goddesses 12, *17*, 22, 23, *26-7*, *40*
gold **15**, 53, *74*
   treasure 10, *20*, 22, 27, *34*, *70*
Gold Coast (*now* Ghana) 51, 67, **87**
Golden Horde, Khanate 44, 45
Gorbachev, Mikhail 81, *89*
Goths 25, *34*, **35**
graves and tombs 9, 10, *21*, *22*
   catacombs *29*
   China 10, *19*
   Egypt *14*, *15*
   Taj Mahal **59**
   Vikings 36, *37*
Great Britain *see* Britain
Great Colombia **73**
Great Khan 44, **45**
Great Trek 66
Great Zimbabwe 27, *46*, **47**
Greece 76, **77**, **83**, 85
   Classical 5, 22-3, **23**, **25**
   Minoans and Mycenaeans 10, **11**, *22*
Greenland 36-7, **37**
Guam 67
Guatemala **73**
guillotine *70*
Guinea **87**
Guinea Bissau 87
Gulf War, oil pollution 89
Guomindang (Kuomintang) 67, **79**, 80
Gupta Empire/dynasty (India) 26
Guyana **73**

H
Habsburg dynasty 55, 66
Haile Selassie, emperor of Ethiopia 80
Hamburg 27
Hammurabi, king of Babylon 11, *13*, **13**
Han Empire/dynasty (China) 18, 26
Handel, George F. *51*
Hangzhou 43
Hannibal, General 25
Hanseatic League 27
Hao **19**
Harappa 11, 16-17, **17**
Hausaland **47**, 66
Hawaii **7**
   Pearl Harbor 67, 84
Hawkins, Sir John 50
Henry II, king of England 27
Herculaneum 26
Herodotus 5
hieroglyphs *see* writing, picture
Himeji *63*, **63**
Hinduism 17, 86, 90
Hiroshima *80*, 85

Hitler, Adolf 84, *85*, **85**
Hittite Empire 11
Holland *see* Netherlands
Holy Roman Empire 26, **39**, 51, **55**, **58**
Homo sapiens 6-7
Homo sapiens sapiens 6, **7**
Honduras 73
Hong Kong 66, *78*, **79**, 81
Hopewell culture 11
hoplites 22
houses 9, 10, *10*, 27, 34
   Roman *24*, 25
   tents *45*
   underground 10, 27
Huari 26
Huguenots 50, 51
Hull **69**
human beings, first 6, **7**
Hundred Years War 27
Hungary 38, **39**, 51, 66, **85**
Huns *34*, **35**
hunting *6*, *7*, *14*

I
Iceland 36, **37**
Idaho 75
Ife culture 27
Ilkhanate of Persia 44
Illinois **75**
Illyrian Province **71**
Inca Empire 27, 48, *49*, **49**, *50*, **52**, 53
India 9, 10-11, 26, 40, **41**
   British colony 50, 51, 53, *64*, **64-5**, 67
   Magadha 11, 16, **17**, 26
   Mughal (Mogul) Empire 50, 51, 58, **59**, 64
   wins independence *86*, **87**
Indian Mutiny (1857) 67
Indiana 75
Indians *see* Native Americans
Indies *see* East Indies; West Indies
Indonesia (East Indies) 51, **65**, 87
Indus Valley civilization 10, *11*, 16, **17**
Industrial Revolution *68*, **69**, 76
Iowa 75
Iran (Persia) 81
Iraq 81, 89
Ireland 9, **37**, 39
   modern 81, 85, 88
iron *see* metalworking
Isabella, queen of Spain 52
Islam 26, 32, 46, 86, 90
Islamic Empire 32, **33**, **37**, **44**, **45**
   see also Mughal Empire; Ottoman Empire; Safavid Empire
Israel
   kingdom of 11
   modern 80-1, *87*
Istanbul 30, 31, **59**

Italy 67, **71**
  African colonies 67, 80
  medieval **35**, **37**
  modern 76, **77**, **83**, 84,
    85, 88
  Roman 25, **25**
Ivan III, prince of
  Moscovy 56
Ivan IV (the Terrible),
  Tsar 56
Ivory Coast **87**

J

Jamaica **52**
Janissaries *50*, *58*, 66
Japan 50, 62-3, **63**
  early history 9, 26, **41**
  samurai 27, **51**, *62*
  takes Taiwan **61**, 67,
    78, **79**
  wars 67, 80, 84, *85*
Jassy, Treaty of 66
Java **41**, **65**
Jayavarman VII,
  Emperor 27
Jericho 81
Jerusalem 20, **21**, **29**, **31**
Jesus Christ 28
Jews 11, 20, 28, 80, *84*
  diaspora 26, 54
  modern Israel 80-1, *87*
Jianguang **41**
Jin, kingdom **43**
Jin, Western (Chinese
  dynasty) 18
John, king of England 27
Jordan 81
Juan Carlos, king of
  Spain 81
Judah, kingdom 11
  Judea 28, **29**
Julius Caesar 11
Justinian, Byzantine
  emperor 26, *30*, **31**
Jutes 35

K

kabuki *62*
Kabul **41**
Kaifeng *42*, **43**
Kalahari desert 7
Kalinga **17**
Kampuchea (Cambodia)
  27, **41**, 81, 87
Kanem-Bornu **47**
Kansas **75**
Karnak **15**
Kasai 51
Kay, John 51
Kazakhstan **57**
Kennedy, John F. 81
Kenya 80, **87**
Kenyatta, Jomo *87*
khans and khanates 44,
  45
Kheperen, king of Egypt
  14
Khmer Empire 27
Khmer Rouge 81
Khomeini, Ayatollah *81*
Kiev 56, **57**
kivas 27
Klerk, Frederik de 81
Knossos, Crete 22

Koran (Quran) *33*, 91
Korea 41, **61**, 67, **79**
Kot-Diji **17**
Kublai (Qubilai) Khan
  27, 44, **45**, 60, 61
Kuwait 81, **87**
Kyonju **41**
Kyoto **63**

L

La Paz **73**
La Venta 11
Lake Maracaibo, battle
  73
Lalibela *46*
Laon *38*
Laos **61**
Lascaux 7
Latin America 72, **73**
  laws *13*, 25
Leeds 69
Lenin, Vladimir *83*
Leo III, Pope 35
Lesotho **87**
letters *20*, 32, 49
Lhasa **41**
Liberia 86, **87**
Libya 11, 67, 80, **87**
Lima **73**
Lincoln, Abraham *75*
Lisbon **55**
Lithuania **39**
Liverpool 69
Livonia **39**
Lo-i *19*
London (*Roman*
  Londinium) *25*, *29*, **39**,
    55, 69, 77, **83**
Longshan culture 10
Lothal **17**
Louis XIV, king of
  France 51, **55**
Louis XVI, king of
  France **55**, 66, *70*
Louis XVIII, king of
  France 66
Louisiana **75**
Lübeck 27
Lunda kingdoms 51
Luofou **41**
Luoyang **41**
Luther, Martin *54*
Luxembourg **77**, 88

M

Macedonians 11
  see also Alexander the
    Great
Machu Picchu *49*, **49**
Madagascar 51, **87**
Madras 51, **64**
Madrid **39**, **55**, **71**, **83**
Magadha
  kingdom 11, 16, **17**
    Gupta Empire 26
Magellan, Ferdinand
  52-3
Magyars (Hungarians)
  38
Mahmud II, Sultan 66
Maine **75**
Malacca **65**
Malawi **87**
Mali **47**, **87**

Manchester **69**
Manchu (Qing) Empire/
  dynasty 51, 60, **61**, 66-
    7, *78*, **79**
Manchuria **61**, 67, **79**
Mandela, Nelson *81*, *86*
Manhattan *51*
Mao Zedong (Mao Tse-
  tung) 80-1, *88*
Maoris (New Zealand)
  66
Maracaibo Lake, battle
  73
Marathas **51**
Marathas (India) 51
Marathon, battle 11, **23**
Marco Polo 43, 44
Marquesas Islands 7
Marseille **29**
Maryland **75**
Massachusetts **75**
Mau Mau (Kenya) 80, 87
Mauritania **87**
Mauryan Empire/
  dynasty 11, 16,
    17, 26
Maya civilization 26, *48*,
  49
Mecca 32, **33**, *59*
medieval Britain 38, **39**
  England 27, **37**, 38, **39**
  invaders **35**, **37**
medieval China 26-7,
  42-3, **43**
medieval Europe 26-7,
  38-9, **39**
Medina 32, **33**, *59*
Mediterranean Sea 11,
  22, **25**
megaliths *9*
Melanesia 7, 10
Memphis 10, **13**, 14, **15**
Menelik, emperor *67*
Menes, king of Egypt 10,
  14
Meroe 26
Mesoamerica 6, **7**, **9**, 10-
  11, 91
  colonization **52-3**, 66
  empires 48-9, **49**
Mesopotamia 10, *12*, *13*,
  13, 26
metalworking *8*, 9, 10
  bronze *8*, 10-11, *18*, 26,
    46
  copper *8*, 10
  iron *8*, 11, 69
  steel *76*
Metternich, Klemens 66
Mexico 10, *73*, 75, 80
Michigan **75**
Middle Ages 26-7, 28-49,
  38-9, **39**
  time-chart 26-7
Middle East, ancient
  history 8, **9**, 10, 12, **13**
Midway Island (US
  base) 67
Milan 38, **39**, **55**
Ming Empire/dynasty
  (China) 51, 60, **61**
Minnesota **75**
Minoan civilization 10,
  11, 22

Minos, king of Crete 22
Mississippi (state) **75**
Mississippi Valley 66, *74*
Missouri **75**
Modern period 66-89
  time-charts 66-7, 80-1
Mogollon culture 27
Mogul *see* Mughal
Mohammad Ali, ruler of
  Egypt 66
Mohenjo-Daro *11*, 16-17,
  17
Moldavia **39**
Moluccas (Spice Islands)
  50, 64, **65**
money *19*
  coins 21, *25*, 32
  paper *42*
Mongke Khan 44
Mongolia 45, **45**, **61**, **79**
Mongols 27, 32, 42, 56
  Mongol Empire 44-5,
    45
Monomotapa *46*, **47**
Montana **75**
Monte Alban
  (Mesoamerica) 11
Montenegro **77**
Montevideo **73**
Morocco 50, 67, **85**, **87**
Moscovy 56
Moscow **39**, 56, 57, **71**
mosques 26, *30*, *32*,
  46
Mosquito Coast **73**
Mozambique **87**
Mugabe, Robert 81
Mughal (Mogul) Empire
  50, 51, 58, **59**, 64
Muhammad 32, 33
Muhammad Ahmad 67
mummies *15*
Mumtaz Mahal 59
Muscovy (Moscovy) **56**
Muslims *see* Islam
Mussolini, Benito 80
Myanmar (Burma) **41**,
  61, **64**
Mycenaean civilization
  11, 22

N

Nagasaki *63*, *80*, *85*
Namibia **87**
Naples **29**, 38, **39**
  kingdom **39**, **55**, **71**
Napoleon Bonaparte 66,
  70, *71*, **71**
  Napoleonic Wars 71
nation states 76, **77**
Native Americans *48*, *52*,
  66, *74*
Navarre, kingdom **39**
Nazca culture 11
Nazi Party 85
Nebraska **75**
Nehru, Jawaharlal 86, *87*
Nemausus (*now* Nimes)
  25
Nepal **61**
Nero, Roman emperor
  29
Netherlands (Holland)
  77, **83**, 84, **85**, 88

Dutch Republic 54, **55**,
  71
  colonies 51, 64, **64-5**,
    66, 74
  Holland under
    Napoleon **71**
  trade 63, 64, *65*
Nevada **75**
New Amsterdam (*now*
  New York) *51*, 74
New Georgia 51
New Granada 72, **73**
New Hampshire **75**
New Hebrides **65**
New Jersey **75**
New Kingdom (Egypt)
  11
New Mexico **75**
New Orleans **75**
New Testament (of
  Bible) *28*, 29
New York (New
  Amsterdam) *51*, 74, **75**
New York (state) **75**
New Zealand **65**, *66*, 80
Newcastle upon Tyne 69
Newfoundland **36**, 51
Nicaragua 67, **73**, 81
Nicholas II, Tsar 67
Niger 66, **87**
Nigeria 11, 27, 80, 86, **87**
  Biafra 81
Nijo *62*, **63**
Nile Valley 10, 11, *12*, **13**
  Red Sea canal 21
  source of River Nile 67
Nimes (*Roman*
  Nemausus) **25**
Nixon, Richard 81
nomads 7, *45*, 91
North Africa 25, 26, *46*,
  47, **55**, 80, *84*
North America
  ancient history 6, **7**, 10,
    11, 26
  found by Europeans
    36, 52
North Carolina 50
North Sea 27
Northern Ireland 81
Northmen (Vikings) **36-7**
Norway **39**, **55**, **71**, 77,
  83, 84, **85**
  Vikings **36**, **37**
Nottingham 69
Nova Scotia 51
Nubia and Nubians 11, **15**
nuclear weapons 80, 81,
  85, 88
Nuremberg rallies 85

O

Ohio **75**
oil fuel 89
Okhotsk **57**
Okinawa Island 85
Oklahoma **75**
Olmecs *11*
Oman 66, **87**
Opium Wars 66, *78*
oracles 91
  Delphi *23*
  oracle bones *18*
Orange Free State 67

94

Oregon **75**
Ortega, Daniel 81
Osaka **63**
Oseberg *36, 37*, **37**
Ostrogoths **35**
Othman, caliph 33
Ottoman Empire 27, 31,
    45
    rise 50, 58, **59**
    slow decline 39, 45, 51,
        55, 66-7, 77, **83**
Oxus River **21**
    treasure 20
Oyo 51

P
Padua 27
Pagan **41**
pagoda 41, *42*
Pakistan 86, **87**
palaces *20, 22, 34, 50*
    Forbidden City *61*
    Versailles *55*
    Winter Palace *56*
Palembang **41**
Palenque 26
Palestine 11, **13**
    Jews 26, 28, 80
    Judea 28, **29**
    West Bank 81, *87*
Panama 67
Papal States **39**, 55
papermaking *42*
Papua New Guinea *50*
Paracas culture 11
Paraguay 72, **73**
Paris 35, 37, 38, **39**, 55, *70*
    nineteenth century **71**,
        76, **77**
    World Wars *80, 82,* **83**,
        85
Park, Mungo 66
Parthian Empire 11
Pataliputra **17**
Patara **29**
Paul, Saint *29*
Pearl Harbor (US base)
    67, 84
Peking (Beijing) *61*, **61**,
    79, 81
Penn, William *51*
Pennsylvania 51, **75**
Persepolis *20, 21*, **21**
Persia (*now* Iran)
    Ilkhanate *44*, **45**
    modern Iran 81
    Safavid Empire 50, 58,
        59
Persian Empire 11, 20,
    21, **23**, 26
    war with Greeks *5*, 11,
        23
    war with Romans 26
Persian Gulf states 66
Perth **65**
Peru *10*, 26, *48, 72*, **73**
Peter the Great, Tsar *56*
pharaohs of Egypt 11
Philippine Is **65**, 67, 87
Phoenician Empire 11,
    24, 25
    Carthage **25**, **29**, **31**, 32
pictograms *see* writing,
    picture

Piedmont *67, 77*
Pizzaro, Francisco 53
plague *39*
Plato, Greek thinker 23
Plymouth **69**
Pol Pot 81
Poland **39**, 55, 56, 77, 89
    Grand Duchy of
        Warsaw **71**
    World Wars 82, **83**, 84,
        85
pollution
    air and water **89**
    fossil fuels **89**
    oil **89**
Polo, Marco 43, 44
Pompeii *25*, **25**, 26
Port Jackson (*now*
    Sydney) **65**
Portsmouth **69**
Portugal 38, 54, **55**, **71**,
    77, **83**, **85**
    colonies *50*, **52-3**, **64-5**,
        66, 72, **73**
    trade and exploration
        27, 52-3, 62, 64, 66
postal systems *20*, 32, 49
pottery *8, 9, 11*
    porcelain (china) *61*
Prague **55**
prehistory 6-9
    time-chart 10
Protestants 50, 54, 91
Prussia 51, **71**
pueblos 27
Puerto Rico 67
Punic Wars 11, 24, 25
Puyo **41**
pyramids *10, 14, 26, 41,*
    48

Q
Qatar **87**
Qin Empire/dynasty 11,
    18, *19*, **19**
Qing (Manchu)
    Empire/dynasty 51,
    60, **61**, 66-7, 78, **79**
Qubilai (Kublai) Khan
    27, 44, **45**, 60, 61
Quebec 50
Quito *49*, **73**
Quran (Koran) *33*, 91

R
Rabin, Yitzhak 81, **87**
railways **69**, *69, 72*, **75**
Raleigh, Sir Walter 50
Rangpur **17**
Ravenna 34, **35**
Recceswinth, King 34
Reformation 50, 54, 91
religions *see* Buddhism;
    Christianity;
    Hinduism; Islam
religious buildings *see*
    churches; mosques;
    temples
religious monuments *9*,
    10, 12
Renaissance *27*, 91
revolutions 66
    French *70, 76*
Rhode Island **75**

Rhodesia (*now* Zambia/
    Zimbabwe) 80-1
Ricci, Mateo *60*
Rio de Janeiro **73**
roads 19, 20, **21**, *49, 63*
Roanoke 50
rock edicts 17
Roman Empire 11, 24-5,
    25, 26, **29**
    see also Byzantine
        Empire; Holy
        Roman Empire
    barbarians 34, **35**
    Christians 29
Romania 77, *83*, **85**, 89
Rome *39*, 55, *71*, 83
    Roman Empire 11, **25**,
        29
    seized by Gauls/
        Goths 11, 34
    under Byzantine/
        barbarian rule **31**,
        32, 35
Rosetta Stone 11
Rothenburg *38, 39*
Ruhr Valley *68*
Rus (*later* Russia) 36, 37,
    56
Russia *37*, 44, **45**, 51, 55,
    59, 77
    becomes Christian 30
    expands and colonizes
        56-7, *57*, **57**, 66, *78*
    goes to war *71*, **71**, 77
    Soviet Union 81, 84,
        86, 87, 88, *89*
    World Wars **82-5**, *83*,
        84, 85
Ruzhen tribes (Jin) **43**
Rwanda **87**

S
Safavid Empire/dynasty
    58, **59**
Sahara, Western **87**
Sahara desert 46, *47*, **47**
    Tuaregs 66, 67
Saint Helena **71**
Saint Petersburg *56*, **77**
Saladin, Emperor 27
Salamis 23
Salvador, El **73**
Samarra 26
samurai 27, *51, 62*
San Martín, José de 72
Sanchi 11
Sandinistas 81
Santiago **73**
Saqqarah *10*
Saracens 38
Sardinia *25*, **29**, **31**, 55,
    77
Sardis *20*, **21**
Sargon, king of Agade
    10, **13**
Sassanian Empire/
    dynasty (Persia) 26
satraps 21
Savoy 55
Saxons (Anglo-Saxons)
    35
Saxons (Germany) 26,
    34, **35**
scholars *23, 33, 48*

science 33, 42, 50, 51, *54*,
    88
Scotland **39**, 69
"Sea Peoples" (Middle
    East) 11
seals (personal) *16*
Second World War 84, **85**
Segovia *24*, **25**
Selim I, Ottoman
    emperor 59
Seljuk (Turkish) Empire
    27
Senegal **87**
Serbia 82, *83*, **85**
Seville **29**
Shah Jahan, Mughal
    emperor 59
Shaka, king of Zulus 66
Shang Empire/dynasty
    (China) 11, 18, *19*, **19**
Shanghai *79*
Sheffield **69**
Shetland Islands *37*
Shi Huangdi, king of
    Qin 18, 19
ships *11, 22, 37, 64, 74*
shogun *62*
Siam (*now* Thailand) **41**,
    61, **65**
Siberia *57*, **57**
Sicily *25*, **29**, **31**, 55, **77**
Sierra Leone 66, **87**
Singapore **65**
Sinkiang 61
Six Day War 81
slavery **31**, 50, 51, 66, 75
    "white slaves" *68*
Slavs 26, **31**, **35**, 56
Slovakia **85**
Smuts, Jan 80
Smyrna **29**
Society Islands **7**
Socrates, Greek thinker
    11, 23
Sofala *47*
soil
    fertile *8, 9, 12, 14, 18*
    loss of fertility *16*
soldiers *see* armies
Solomon, king of Israel
    11
Somalia (Somaliland) 80,
    87
Somme, battle *83*
Song Empire/dynasty
    (China) 27, *42*, **43**
Songhai *47*, 50
South Africa 66-7
    Boer War 67
    diamonds found 67
    modern 80-1, *86*, **87**
    Zulu kingdom 66
South America
    ancient history *6*, **7**, **9**,
        10, 11
    colonization **52-3**
    end of colonies 66, 72,
        73
South Carolina **75**
Southampton **69**
Soviet Union 81, 84, 86,
    87, 88, *89*
    see also Russia
Spain 55, **71**, **77**, **83**, **85**, 88

colonies *50*, **52-3**, *66-7,*
    72, **73**
    medieval 34, **35**, **37**, *39*,
        54
    Roman *24*, **25**
Sparta 22
Speke, John 67
Sphinx, the *14*
Spice Islands (*later*
    Moluccas) 50, 64, **65**
Sri Lanka (Ceylon) 40,
    41, *64, 77*
Stalingrad (*now*
    Volgograd), battle *84*,
    85
Stephenson, George 69
steppe *45*
Stockholm 55
Stockton and Darlington
    Railway *69*
Stone Age 6-7, *9, 10*
stone pillars (inscribed)
    11, *13*, 17
Stonehenge *9*
stonemason *39*
Strasbourg *88*
stupa *11, 26, 41*, 91
Sudan 11, **87**
Suez Canal 80
sufi *32*
Suleiman the
    Magnificent *50*, 51, 59
Sumatra **41**, **65**
Sumer (*modern* Iraq) 11,
    12
    temple/emperor *10*
Sun Yat-sen 67
superpowers *88*, 91
Susa *20*, **21**
Suzhou *43*, **43**
Swahili culture 27
Swaziland **87**
Sweden **39**, 55, **71**
    modern period 77, *83*,
        85
    Viking period 36, *37*
Switzerland **71**, *83*, **85**
    Swiss Confederation
        55
Sydney (Port Jackson) **65**
Syria 11, **13**, **23**, *59*, 81

T
taiga *57*
Taiwan (Formosa) **61**, 67,
    78, **79**
Taj Mahal *59*
Tang dynasty (China) 26,
    42
Tanganyika **87**
Tangier 30, *32*
Tannenberg, battle *83*
Tasman, Abel **65**
Tasmania (Van Diemen's
    Land) **65**
taxes *15, 60, 70, 74, 78*
    tribute *21*, **21**
tea-pickers *77*
technology *6*, **7**, *42*
    flight *67*
    gasoline engine *68, 76*
    metalworking *9*
        bronze *8*, 10-11, *18*,
            26, 46

95

copper 8, 10
iron and steel 8, 11, 69, *76*
mills and factories 38, *68, 69*
pottery *8, 9, 11, 61*
steam engine 68, *69, 72*
weaving *10, 48,* 51
wheel *8*
Temple Mound culture 26
temples *10, 11, 48*
mosques *26, 30, 32, 46*
pagoda *40, 41, 42*
stupa *11, 26, 41*
Temuchin *see* Chinghiz Khan
Tennessee **75**
Tenochtitlán 27
Teotihuacán 26, 48, **49**
Texas **75**
textiles *10, 48,* 51, *68,* **69**
Thailand (Siam) **41, 61, 65**
theater, Japanese *62*
Thebes **13**, 15
Thermopylae **23**
Thessalonica **25, 31, 31**
thinkers *17, 23,* 40, 54
Thirty Years War 50, 54, 55
Tianjin 79
Tibet **41, 45, 61, 79**
Tigris Valley 11, **13,** 26
Tikal 26
time-charts
4000 BC-1 BC (ancient civilizations) 10-11
AD 1-1500 (the Middle Ages) 26-7
AD 1500-1750 (empires around the world) 50-1
AD 1750-1913 (industry and revolution) 66-7
AD 1914-2000 (twentieth century) 80-1
Tinne, Alexandrine 67
Togo **87**
Tokugawa shoguns 62-3
Tokyo (Edo) **63**
Toledo, Spain **32**
Toltec Empire 26-7
tombs *see* graves and tombs
tools *see* technology
Tordesillas, Treaty of **53**
towns *see* cities and towns
toys and games *16, 48, 49*
trade 10, 11, 21
Africa 27, 46-7
East India companies 64, 67
Europe–Asia 52, 61, 63, 78
European colonies 50-1, 64
medieval 37, 38, 42, 44
prevented *63·*

Trajan, Roman emperor **25**
transport *9, 11, 22, 26*
automobiles *76*
camel caravans *47*
canals 21, *43,* **43, 69**
letters *20,* 32, 49
railways *69,* **69,** *72,* **75**
ships 11, 22, 37, 52, 64, *74*
space travel *81*
Transvaal 67
travel and exploration **36-7,** *52-3*
treasure 22, 27, 34, *70*
Oxus 20
Varna 10
treaty ports 78, **79**
trench warfare 82
Trevithick, Richard 69
tribute (tax in kind) *21,* 21
Trinidad 52
Tripoli **47**
tsar (csar, czar) 90
Tuaregs 66, 67
Tudor and Stuart England 50-1
Tunisia 80, **87**
Turfan **41**
Turkey and Turks 45, *80,* **85**
Ottoman Empire 27, 31, 45
rise 50, 58, **59**
slow decline **39,** 45, 51, **55,** 66-7, **77, 83**
Seljuk Empire 27

U
Uganda 81, **87**
Ukraine 56
Umayyad Empire/ dynasty 32, **33**
the Union (USA) 75
United Arab Emirates **87**
United Kingdom (Britain and Ireland) **77**
United Nations 81
United States of America 66-7, 74, **75**
buys Alaska 57
Civil War 67, *75*
colonization of 66, 74
influence 63, 67, 86, 87, 88
slavery 66, *67*
trade 67, 69
World Wars 80, 82, 83, 84, *85*
Ur 12, **13**
king *13*
Ural Mountains 57
Uruguay 72, **73**
Utah **75**
Uttarapatha **17**

V
Van Diemen's Land (*now* Tasmania) **65**
Vandals 25, 34, **35**
Vargas, Getulio 80
Varna, Bulgaria 10
Venezuela 72, **73**

Venice 38, **39,** 50, **55**
Verdun, battle *82,* **83**
Vermont **75**
Vesalius, Andreas 54
Vespucci, Amerigo 52
Vesuvius, Mount 25, 26
viceroy 52
Victoria, Lake 67
Victorian Britain 68, **69,** 76, **77**
Vienna 58, **77, 83**
siege by Turks 51, *58*
Vietnam 80-1
Vikings 36, 36, **37, 37**
villages 8, 9, 10
Japan 62
Viking *36*
Virginia **75**
Visigoths 35
Vladimir, prince of Kiev 30
volcanic eruptions 25, 26
Volga River **56**
Volgograd *see* Stalingrad

W
Wales
industry **69**
stone for Stonehenge 9
Wall Street crash 80
walls
Baghdad **44**
Berlin 81, **89**
Constantinople 31
Great Wall of China *19,* 42, 60
Hadrian's Wall 25
Zimbabwe *46*
wars
of independence 72-3, 74
of religion 33, 50, 54, 58, 59
over colonies 51
Warsaw **39, 55, 71**
Washington, DC **75**
Washington, George 66, *75*
Washington (state) **75**
water supplies 24
Watergate scandal 81
Waterloo, battle **71**
Watt, James 68
weapons and armor, 22, 31, 44, 45, 49, 51, 62
modern *82–5*
tank 83
weaving *10, 48,* 51, 68
Wessex, kingdom 37
West Bank (of Jordan) 81
West Indies 50, 52
West Virginia **75**
Western Sahara **87**
westernization 56, *78*
resisted 61, 62
Westphalia 71
Treaty of 55
Whitby **69**
William I, duke of Normandy 27
Wisconsin **75**
Wolverhampton 69
women at work *82*
World Wars
First 82, **83**
Second 84, **85**
writing 22, *28*

picture 11, *12, 13, 15, 16,* 90
Wyoming **75**

X
Xerxes, king of Persia 20, 23
Xi'an **19**
Xinjiang *60,* **61, 79**
Xixia, kingdom **43**

Y
Yangshao culture 10
Yangtze River **19,** 79
Yellow River (Huang Ho) 11, *18,* **19**
Yenisei River **57**
York (*Roman* Eboracum) **25,** 69
Ypres, battle **83**
Yuan Empire/dynasty 44
Yugoslavia 81

Z
Zaire (Belgian Congo) 67, **87**
Zambia **87**
Zanzibar 66
Zapotecs 11
Zhou dynasty (China) 11
ziggurat of Ur *12*
Zimbabwe 81, **87**
Great 27, 46, **47**
Zulus 66

Index by Gerard M-F. Hill

Acknowledgments

The publishers would like to thank the following for the use of their pictures:
Bridgeman Art Library is indicated as **BAL**
Christine Osborne Pictures is indicated as **COP**
E. T. Archive is indicated as **ETA**
Hulton Getty Picture Collection is indicated as **HGC**
Mary Evans Picture Library is indicated as **MEPL**
Robert Harding Picture Library is indicated as **RHPL**
SCALA Istituto Fotografico Editoriale (Firenze) is indicated as **S**
Sonia Halliday Photographs is indicated as **SHP**
Tony Stone Images is indicated as **TSI**
Werner Forman Archive is indicated as **WFA**
ZEFA Pictures is indicated as **Z**

Front cover *top* BAL *bottom left* RHPL *middle* Z *right* Ashmolean Museum, Oxford; back cover *left* Bibliothèque Nationale de France *middle* TSI *right* MEPL; page 1 TS; page 3 ETA; page 7 *top* Colorphoto Hans Hinz, Allschwil-Basel SWB *middle* SHP; p8 *left* SHP *right* Steiermärkisches Landesmuseum, Joanneum; p9 SHP; p12 *both* RHPL; p13 BAL; p14 *left* Z *right* RHPL; p15 BAL; p16 *left* Explorer, Paris *right* C M Dixon; p17 Ashmolean Museum, Oxford; p18 *both* RHPL; p19 RHPL; p20 *left* BAL *right* COP; p21 RHPL; p22 *left* Z *right* BAL; p23 TS/R Everts; p24 *left* S *right* TSI; p25 Z; p28 *left* The John Rylands University Library, University of Manchester *right* Z/G Hell; p29 S; p30 *left* RHPL *right* ETA; p31 WFA; p32 TSI; p33 *left* ETA *right* WFA; p34 *left* S *right* Z; p36 *left* BAL *right* C M Dixon; p37 WFA; p38 *left* Z *right* RHPL; p39 Bibliothèque Royale Albert 1er, Bruxelles; p40 *left* Z *right* ETA; p41 RHPL; p42 *left* RHPL *right* Andromeda Oxford Limited; p43 RHPL; p44/45 Z/J Bitsch; p45 Bibliothèque Nationale de France, Paris; p46 *left* RHPL *right* WFA/B Heller/R Aberman; p47 SHP; p48 *left* TSI *right* Z/Janoud; p49 TSI; p52 BAL; p53 BAL; p54 *left* BAL/Giraudon *right* BAL; p55 BAL; p56 Z; p57 Z; p58 SHP; p59 Z; p60 *left* ETA *right* RHPL; p61 RHPL; p62 *left* WFA *right* TSI; p63 TSI; p64 ETA; p65 ETA; p68 *left* Archiv Gerstenberg, Wietze, Germany *right* MEPL; p69 Peter Newark's Pictures; p70 *left* MEPL *right* HGC; p71 Giraudon, Paris; p72 *both* South American Pictures/M. & T. Morrison; p73 South American Pictures/M. & T. Morrison; p74 *left* BAL *right* Z; p75 Peter Newark's Pictures; p76 *left* HGC *right* MEPL; p77 HGC; p78 *both* MEPL; p79 Peter Newark's Pictures; p82 *both* Imperial War Museum, London; p83 HGC; p84 *left* Novosti *right* National Archives, Washington D.C.; p85 Imperial War Museum, London; p86 *both* HGC; p87 Associated Press; p88 *left* European Parliament *right* ETA; p89 Frank Spooner Pictures.
Picture research by Anne Lyons